POWER
SUCCEED

Elliot Kay

Power To Succeed

Copyright © 2015 Elliot Kay

ISBN: 978-1542889599

Testimonials

"It helped me make my peace with myself and let go of the blame and guilt I carried for years via a simple exercise of writing a letter. It connected me to some amazing people and gave me one of the most powerful affirmations to kick-start my day: 'I command my subconscious mind to allow me to show up in certainty.' – Thank you Elliot Kay."
– Melissa E Butt, NLP practitioner.

"It's improved my relationship with myself. I've come a long way from the serious guy who first joined. Meeting you that day was one of the best things that has ever happened to me, period."
– Sukbinder Bhatia, youth coach.

"Last year, I was about to be sacked from my job. I had no focus and I was drifting waiting for things to happen. Since Power to Succeed, I am the top performer in my office, lead on different projects and have a prestigious new job. Thanks for all your support."
– Graham McCabe, career consultant.

"Helped me to tune into my passion, connect to people, accept my journey and life in various aspects, grow as an individual and be more of service to others."
– Jerome Harvey-agyei, motivational speaker.

Contents

Waking Up After Living Someone Else's Dream…

"Elliot, I'm fed up with waking up and living someone else's dream every single day." If only I had a pound for every time I have heard that.

Carl woke up resentful, angry and feeling very heavy. Soon the anger numbed out. It was normally on the way home from work, it became sadness, and he started to question why he did this to himself every single day. Carl would always find the strength to keep going; yet somehow it always felt like he was burning the candle at both ends. Carl simply knew that something else awaited him. He wasn't sure what it was, but he knew it was there. Yet every day he chose to get up, tired and dispirited, put his mask of smiles on and go to build a business that he had lost the passion for. Every day working with someone who he didn't connect with or agree with on a business level. The person he was working with was a friend, yet to work with was a nightmare.

Do you know someone like that? Could this be where you are right now as you read this book? Are you in a place where you know there is greatness in you? You simply are stuck in the mundane day-to-day living, yet with no actual life? Are you like Carl feeling that this is the only way and are afraid to step away into the unknown because it might not work out? You might fail? You don't have the skills? Or maybe you have excellent friendships in your workplace, but the job itself is making you miserable?

That was Carl, all of the above and more. Because Carl was in such a conflicted place in his mind, it was no surprise that the relationships that he found himself in were also very destructive and he couldn't find a way out of them. When we started working together, Carl met a woman that would be demanding, possessive and slightly nutty. When Carl picked up the phone to me, he was broken, emotionally on his knees and in despair! He contacted me about his relationship (something I don't always work with) and wanted some coaching around how to deal with the girl he was seeing, who was choking him emotionally. At this point, we didn't look at his situation in life generally. As I had met him before, I was more than happy to work with him and support him – but on one condition: "Whatever we agree in the session, you must DO with no excuses." He agreed. When we met, he was nervous and pale as he didn't know what he was letting himself in for. He had heard from others that I was the person to go to. He was emotionally broken and very lost when we started. Lots of blame was being laid on her, poor girl. I stopped him. "Hang on a minute!" I raised my voice slightly: "What part are you playing in all this, blaming her for everything? What part are YOU playing in this?" He carried on wanting to shift the blame, but I didn't let him. "How are you supporting her behaviour?" The session changed direction, it became about him owning the situation and not the situation owning him. We did some closed eyes situation rehearsal. That's when I take the person into an imaginary rehearsal of a situation. That way when it happens, they are able to deal with it and control themselves better. I use this a lot when I work with people on confidence and social anxiety. This is one of many things I can do using Cognitive Behavioural Hypnotherapy training. We also did some processes to release the emotional charge and to relax him. He suddenly stopped midway through the session. His look lightened up, his colour returned to his face, it was as if years of hardship were lifted. "I need to end it," he said. "Are you sure that's not just running away?" I asked. "NO, Elliot, it is for the best for me and her, better to be free of each other now than hoping it will work out while holding each other's throats."

We then did some work on confidence. The deal was he would end the relationship that night and call me. I was very happy to see his name flash up on the screen two hours later. "Elliot, I have a wet face, a wet shirt, and I am still in the restaurant." You know those scenes in movies when the guy tells the girl he doesn't want to see her any more and she picks up her glass and throws it at the guy? It turns out Carl had experienced that firsthand when he broke up with her. Here is the interesting thing. "Elliot, normally I would run after her and feel guilty. This time I just asked for a napkin, carried on with my drink, paid and left." That was just the beginning of Carl's journey: a journey which would lead him to leave his miserable situation with his job to become an in-demand photographer setting up Inspired By Reality Photography working with celebrities, Amazon and many more companies.

Here I am, Elliot Kay – widely known as The Coach with

the Hat. I am owner of two different companies and a commercial director of another. I have worked with Olympic athletes, start-ups, business owners and many more people. My area of expertise is being at your best at all times through dealing with the challenges that go with it, that is what Peak Performance is all about. I do this through a variety of training methods and products. I work with people to be at their best at all times, mainly in the entrepreneurial space, both strategically and emotionally. I have written two books, launched two different seminars and recently my successful Power To Succeed Seminar having helped thousands of people move out of their jobs, launch businesses and simply find their path. People I worked with kept commenting how much they loved my first book. "Elliot I loved your first book, when is the next one out?" "Elliot when will you package your seminar into a book?" This question kept coming up. After such extensive requests, I decided to write my third book. I decided to write this to reach more people like yourself who I might not have met, or who wanted a little bit of a taster into who I am and what I do. I sat down and thought of why I should go through the process of writing a book for the third time. What value would it add? I had grown a lot, learned and worked with so many more people from since I wrote my first two books that it felt right. In fact, I have worked with well over 3,000 people in the last two years alone. It felt right because I have strength in my voice and in my message. It was time to extend my reach and share more of my message with you. It felt right because I was and am getting great feedback on my first book It's

Your Right to be Wrong. It felt right because doing advanced training with my students demanded it of me. I am teaching them how to write a book, so isn't it time I came out with a new one?

I have seen a lot in my years as a coach. I have clients in Spain, Germany, and have worked with people in the USA, Australia, Rwanda and Israel. I have people fly in to attend my seminars from Poland, Israel and Romania. I have worked with people who are massively wealthy and with people who have very little. With over 10 years as a trainer, I have trained for the likes of Sky Television, TalkTalk and The NHS. I have spoken in front of thousands of people both nationally and internationally. My message is loud and clear, and I can stand in front of pretty much anyone and deliver it.

From a business angle, there are always a lot of assumptions around people who appear to be successful. A lot of the time people assume it is easy or things simply landed in their lap. I used to think that it only happened to certain people and not to people like me. Do you know anyone who might do that? Do you know anyone who thinks and feels that success is only for the privileged few? Allow me to share with you right now and throughout the entire book. My journey to finding success has certainly been the most challenging experience. I have seen my ups come crashing down; I have seen myself lay there at night, wide awake, looking up at the ceiling wondering how I am going to pay the rent with that feeling of utter desperation, heart beating fast and very loud voices in my head telling me to give up. Laying there even questioning if it is worth to keep going. Pondering on the notion of giving up. You know those days when the voices that are loudest in your head appear to be ones you listen to? The one that are telling you to play it safe, that you gave it a go and it is time to give up? Those are the voices I am glad I ignored.

It was the end of February 2011, I had been back from Australia for a month. Broke after watching myself lose everything that I thought was important to me. (More about this to follow later.) I had no idea how I would be paying the rent that was due the next day. I had nothing in my account. I woke up that morning with my gut telling me that things were about to change. "February is ending. It will all change," my gut kept telling me. My head was another matter. I got out of bed looking for where I could get the money to pay my rent. "Who can I borrow from?", "What will people think if I ask them for rent money?" "Fuck why am I here?" The voices and questions kept getting louder and louder. Then my mobile rang; I will never forget it, it was at exactly noon. "Elliot, we have lost a trainer and we need someone who can step in and deliver with very little notice. Can you do it?" It was my old employer. "Of course I can," I said, containing my relief and happiness. "As you don't work for us any more, what would be your daily rate?" I gave them my daily rate, which was three times what I would have been paid if I had worked there. Then there was a pause, a silence that felt like it went on forever. Already the voices were kicking in, "You fool, it was too much, you should have just taken what they offered, you are a fool!" Then I heard it: "Elliot, that is fine, we will pay that amount. Can we book you for the month?" And that was it. I could pay my rent and brought in a few thousand pounds to get me through. I came off the phone and did a dad dance across the living room. You know what I mean? Something like the "running man" and a poor version of 'Riverdance.' Then I burst into tears for a few minutes. Relief and joy, what a great combination. I started the next day. Have you ever been there? Stuck wondering where you next break is going to come from?

Towards the end of the month, the training manager sat me down and said, "Elliot, we need you back. We love what you do and how you do it. We will pay treble your salary from what we paid you last time, you in?" I had no hesitation in coming back to her and saying, "no". No matter how broke I was, I left that place to build my future, and I wasn't willing to compromise on that. Brave or stupid, there is a fine line. You know, sometimes in life we are given a choice: short-term fix or long-term gain. What would you have chosen?

That became a bit of a trend. I won a few more contracts, and each time I found myself turning down around £60K a year jobs while having very little in the bank. Brave or stupid? This is why it is time to write this book. Throughout the book, I will be sharing with you how I turned my situation around. If I can do it, you can do it too. This book is for you to share my learnings, for you to implement them into your life. For you to gain your insights, I will go into the depth of my story like never before.

Part of this journey has had its own twists and turns. Even in my darkest days, I never thought people I considered friends would turn their backs on me. People I thought of as good friends betrayed my trust. Information I shared in confidence was shared like Christmas cards. As a result, people avoided me in the street and gossiped behind my back. Suddenly, I was considered to be competition to them or not needed as a friend. That hurt. Has that happened to you? Have you been in a similar situation? Maybe you are going through something like that right now? Perhaps you are wondering: why me? My question is how can you turn things around to your advantage? Keep working till you end up grateful. That's how I feel today. Grateful.

It's with gratitude I look back at that now, because it simply drove me to work harder and protect my reputation even more. You may be in a similar situation right now, or perhaps feeling desperate and despairing. Let me reassure you. Sometimes when life is tough, this is when it is offering you the biggest blessings and lessons. I realise that now, and I am confident that one day you will see the same thing too. I have been through the experience of going personally bankrupt. While my business was doing well, I personally was going through bankruptcy because of doing the right thing at the wrong time. Ever done that? The right thing at the wrong time? I used my personal finances and borrowed to make it work, which, sadly, it didn't. The last two years started with me in Australia, in love, thinking I was starting something new but instead that turned out to be the beginning of a sharp fall and slow recovery.

Now, I can share with you all the tools that got me through those times and beyond; I can sit here with a strong message and stand up on stage and deliver my talks and seminars. Hand on heart, I speak from experience. I have lost £150,000 in an investment. At one point, I lost all my clients. Now I pull in thousands a month while growing one of the most exciting coaching companies to come out of the UK, thanks to my experience and what happened to me when everything went wrong. Maybe you know what it is like to fall into a massive hole of debt? Or see something you built crumble in front of your eyes, while feeling powerless? Perhaps you have lost more than me, perhaps less. But I know the sum makes no difference. You can still recover, always, as long as you can open your eyes the next day and breathe, you have another chance.

This is why it is time for me to write this book. I am writing this book because people have asked me to do it, and not to write the book would be short-changing people of the tools I use and my message. What I am doing is simply sharing what has worked for me, and what works for others who have been coached by me and worked with me in my seminars. Now, a lot of them run successful businesses. I have worked with people who started off with a small concept of a business idea but are now running six-figure turnover businesses. I have seen people come in broke with no money to get the dream job they wanted. I have worked with people who were struggling with their business and changed their strategy to multiply their services and turnover.

I have studied and worked with many teachers, all the while I have come up with my own way of saying and conveying the message that you have the power to succeed.

Another reason I wanted to write the book is because what you are going to read in this book works as long as you apply and live in the action. This isn't another self-development book, about the law of attraction that will encourage you to sit and simply wait for what you want. This book is all about getting up from your backside and taking action, directed action and focused action. If you simply want to sit there hoping, wishing, and daydreaming, please close the book and use it to slap yourself across the face. Then, when you are willing to take action, carry on reading. This book is about creating and getting what you want. That does mean taking action. By the way, sitting on your backside doing nothing is still taking action; it is simply taking the action of non-action. I will say this again: if you are going to sit on your backside and do nothing after reading this book, stop reading now.

I am picky regarding who I work with one-on-one as a coach, and I will convey the same message here; this book is for those of you who are committed to facing the pain and challenges in your life; this book is for those who want to go deep and face their past trauma; this book is for those who want to create long-lasting change in their lives and not pipe dreams or what I call Hollywood, which can be anything between a delusion or fantasy, something that isn't real yet you invest a lot of energy in some hope that it will bring you success quickly and effortlessly.

This book is for people who are willing to invest in themselves for the long term. My question to you is: is that you? Because if you are none of the above, please hand this book to someone who will take action and use what is in it; otherwise, you are disrespecting the amount of work that has gone into writing this book, you are disrespecting my experiences, and, more importantly, you are disrespecting yourself. By reading every single page of this book, doing the exercises you will gain clarity, you will learn some great tools to help you deal with the emotional side of starting a business, and you will have some very clear goals to implement. You will gain insight into how I did it and how you can do it too.

I want you to understand this might appear a lot to ask; understand that I strongly believe I am so incredibly lucky. It is because of what I share in this book that I am able to stand on stage and run my seminars; because of my experiences that I share in this book, I coach and work with people. I do this to help as well as support people to have better businesses, careers and lives. It is because of all this that I have undying desire and drive. It is because of my story I have been on the most amazing journey that had me coming 3rd in Britain's Next Top Coach, develop The Empowering Coaching Systems and run experiential seminars. I have delivered over 5,000 hours of talks that are increasing all the time and I developed a really cool coaching brand The Coach with the Hat.

This doesn't mean that challenge doesn't exist or won't ever. This doesn't mean I never get it wrong. It means that now I have a range of tools that I use when life throws challenges at me and now I get to share them with you. Wouldn't it be great for you to be able to look at all the challenges you have had, and will have, and think, 'What a blessing!'

Ever Wanted to Give Up?

In all my years as a dancer (I will tell you more about that later), trainer and coach I have come to learn the main reasons why people give up on their journeys. Theo Paphitis, the serial entrepreneur and former BBC dragon says that 50% of start-ups fail within the first two years. That is an alarming statistic. Department of Trade and Industry & VAT statistics show that just under 70% (68.9%) of VAT-registered businesses cease to trade within ten years of registering for VAT.[1] That doesn't include businesses that don't reach the VAT threshold. Why do entrepreneurs give up or sometimes never start their journey? After all, isn't failing just a part of success? The thought of so many people giving up makes me really sad. How many potentially great ideas, innovative products and great services never make it to light? Is it lack of education? Is it lack of knowledge? Is it because you were born in the wrong family? Environment? Race? Colour? Religion? Failed in the past? Failed a few times in the past? Don't have the right skills? Were born poor? Were born rich?

You see, it is a myth that you need an education or even need to know how to get going. I spent two years going from seminar to seminar, looking for the secret. I wanted each person on stage, the business mentor, the motivational

---

[1] (http://www.financialpreneur.com/?p=41)

speaker to give me the "missing ingredient" or the "secret to success." There are some incredible teachers and seminars out there. I learnt a great deal from going to all these seminars and from being a part of the crew. I learnt so much, I built a business around it. However, there was no secret. There comes a stage when you need education, as well as knowledge and money. However, this is not necessary at the start. Most people get going and reach a certain stage where they come into judgement, a stage where you taste failure when you wonder, "why bother?" The difference between people that keep going and the people that don't is the following:

No coach

The role of a coach is often underestimated and often overlooked, especially in the U.K. A lot of people give up because they don't have a coach to help, support and guide them through the journey. There are times when you need support, and there are times when you need an ass kick. There are a lot of coaches out there, yet people choose not to turn to one because of the stigma that it is weak to seek help or that you can do it alone. I will tell you now that is a myth and pretty much a doomed journey. If it weren't for the coaches I have worked with, I would have given up and gone back to work. It would have taken me a lot longer to turn my business around and build the life I am living now. Which leads me to the next reason.

Isolation

Another reason people give up. We have certain human needs, and they have to be met; it doesn't matter if you study Maslow's *Hierarchy of Needs* or Tony Robbins' *Six Human Needs*. Inherently we have a huge need to belong, a need to be a part of something, and this is one of the biggest drivers of our behaviour. So strong is our need to belong that we will change our behaviour to fit in. We will change our appearance and what it is we want to do in order to fulfil our need to belong. Therefore, if you are starting out on a journey and don't feel that you belong and are on your own, you will stop and look to fulfil your need to belong. Even if that means giving up on your dream. I have seen this time and time again: people giving up on their dreams to please others. While a lot of entrepreneurs do enjoy their own company at times, no person is an island.

No support

Lack of support is another big reason. This isn't to say that your family or friends aren't supportive. It is to say that it isn't the right type of support. In many situations, your friends don't know how to support such a journey, which once again leaves you isolated. Generally speaking, if someone has always been an employee and has done what they were told, and even if they worked their way up, your friends or family would be limited in the support they can offer you. This isn't to say that they aren't supportive in their own way; they can only offer support in the way they know. Which normally means to protect you and tell you to play it safe, get a job or do it their way. So if you are on your journey, you might feel that there is no support and give up. For example, you want a Mercedes. Do you ask the chauffeur or do you ask the owner how to get one? Or you want to invest in property. Do you ask the tenant or the letting agent how to do it, or do you ask the landlord? On the surface, they might seem like they "know" the topic, but in reality they don't. Even if they are involved in the industry, it doesn't mean they know how to build a business from it. It's about having the right support around you.

Consistency

Most give up on their journey to success because they are not consistent. Most people have a half-hearted attempt at creating a success. A little bit like dipping your little toe in the deep and calling it a swim. Sometimes, they might get their full foot in and then simply stop. Some people when wanting to create their life of success might jump in once, but then realise there is a lot more to this journey than meets the eye. That building something with longevity takes time, patience, and focus. You learn that sometimes from jumping in head first. For some people doing nothing appears easier. Is that what you think?

Some people have a go here and there and leave big gaps in between, with very little guidance or education. Then they don't get the results and give up. People attempt to do it alone, with no coach and no support, and then have a little go at creating success and fail. After a few goes, they give up.

Accountability

Another reason why people give up is a very simple concept that is easily overlooked: the element of accountability. In other words, you are held accountable, to a high standard, by someone who makes sure that when you say something you do it. The notion that you have to do everything alone is so old school and seldom works. This is the myth of the self-made millionaire. It does well for marketing purposes, and that's about it. If no one is holding you accountable and making sure that you do what you said you were going to do, you are less likely to do it. We are masters of distraction. How often do we set out to do something brilliant, maybe run a 10k race, but we do a couple of runs and then stop? Maybe it is signing up for the gym because you want to lose weight, but you never seem to find the time to do it? Go to that Salsa class? We are very good as human beings at finding excuses, being distracted and letting ourselves get away with it. What's worse is that we feel guilty about it and beat ourselves up emotionally. Then we don't want to do it, don't want to ask for help and give up.

According to the International Coaching Federation, by simply getting coaching you can increase your work performance by 70%, improve your time management by 57%, and increase your confidence by 80%.[2]

Putting stats aside, you don't have to give up. This whole book is dedicated to making sure you have the tools to keep going. Challenges will always be there. It is how we deal with them that defines us. The choice of keeping going or giving up is as fine as bravery or stupidity. Even if you have given up in the past, it doesn't mean that has to design your future. Even if things haven't worked out in the past, it still means you can rebuild for the future. It's all about the choices we make and acting on them. Learning when to walk away and when to stick is the challenge. I could have walked away from my dream and taken the £60K job. I stuck it out and it has been very rewarding. This is why accountability is such an important element of the process.

---

[2] http://www.coachfederation.org/find-a-coach/benefits-of-coaching/

How Do I Get Started?

There was Beatrix, standing in front of me at the end of my *Power To Succeed* seminar on day one, in tears, wiping her snotty nose. "Elliot, I have had enough. I have spent the whole day crying, and I want to change! I haven't cried like this in years, and it's about time it all came out! I am sick to death of working for people who don't appreciate me and don't have my standards, I want change." "Nice to meet you too, Beatrix, what will you do differently?" I asked. "I don't know, but I know that I will do it." This was the beginning of Beatrix's journey with us. Beatrix joined our advanced training. She was in a very dark place, she had lost her confidence, which meant she came across as blunt when she expressed herself, or said nothing, which was far worse than non-expression. You show me someone who is depressed, and I will show you someone who doesn't express themselves. Beatrix not knowing what to do was perfectly OK. People have this inbuilt program that switches on that says, "You must have all the answers all the time and at once; therefore, you must know what to do and when to do it right away!" There is an expression for that: "Bullshit!" Not knowing is perfectly OK, Beatrix didn't know, and that was a great place to build from. She was willing to explore doing things differently, and, more importantly, was willing to invest her time to make it happen. I remember the first time I invested in coaching. Within two weeks, I spent over £20,000 on self-development, and over time I have made 10 times more than that; when you apply the learning it accelerates your results.

Let's dial back the clock now. I had qualified as a coach and was starting a new journey, and I knew a coach without a coach is a hypocrite. Any coach without a coach – don't touch them! I went to a seminar and found my coach. I was looking for a coach who would develop me as a coach, support me improving as a coach and help me to build a coaching practice. A coach who would hold me accountable for my actions. Who holds *you* accountable right now? We worked together for a few sessions. She gave me lots of support, but I knew one wasn't enough. I went to another seminar and met one of my mentors, someone who is still a mentor today. When I attended his seminar for the first time, I was confronted with a big price tag and this was in 2008. I was speaking to one of his sales team, mostly about 'Transformers' my favourite movie and joining the course. "How much?" I asked. "£15,000," she answered. *'15,000 spondolies? 15,000 fat ones? 15,000 fucking pounds,'* I thought, my heart beating fast, my head going nuts with thoughts. But one underlying question kept popping up: "How the fuck will or can I come up with that amount of money?" I didn't know how, and yes, it was scary, it was a big commitment. Every cell in my body wanted to do this, even though my head was messier than spaghetti junction, I knew this was the right thing to do and had to be done there and then. More than everything, it felt very right. I simply had to make a commitment to make it work and get on the program. "Are there payment plans?"

"Yes, there are." We discussed the *how* and at the end of that night I was on the program, I had put a large deposit down, and I was in. I didn't know how, I did know I wanted to and would make it work. That night I got back to my flat in Acton, West London, and went to sleep. Only to jump in the middle of the night short of breath and in a panic. *What have I done? What I have committed to? I don't have the money?* I stopped myself, took a deep breath in, and set some goals to make it happen.

There are all kinds of schools of thought around goal setting. Some people feel that they can simply live in the flow and, therefore, don't need goals; others set SMART goals. There is one issue with SMART goals. They always seem to create future goals that stay in the future. SMART goals are very effective when doing CBT work and to move the client into solution mode; however, I must admit I am not their greatest fan.

Our belief system, as powerful as it is, will only react to the internal language you feed it. Working with various clients, I have heard many self-statements, even though you might say things intellectually, verbally it's what the internal dialogue says that the unconscious listens to. Self-statements like:

- I am simply not good enough

- I can't make it work

- Who am I to do this (a client favourite)

- I am not born to be successful

- Money doesn't stick around

- If only I had more …

- I don't deserve love

- I will never be …

- They are better than me

Therefore, if goals are set in the future and are intangible, you are telling your belief system that that is where it is going to stay. Your goals will feel distant and unreal. Does this sound familiar? This explains why so many people set goals and don't achieve them. Add to this not dealing with the disempowering belief systems and self-sabotage. While setting goals that aren't in line with their values and aren't tied to a purpose; a purpose that is greater than them. *Meaning* is greater than happiness. Having worked with Olympic athletes, career-driven professionals and entrepreneurs, there are two different effective goal-setting formulas that we use under the Empowering Coaching System, and they are the most effective that I stand by.

Before I go into that, I want to explain about goals: the upside and the downside to setting goals. Like everything else, this has its positives and negatives.

Why set goals?

Goal setting is your first step towards going up a level and increasing achievement. It marks your first point towards success. This is an important part of our strategy; goals are not *the* strategy, but simply part of it. It is like having a moving target that puts you into action mode. The issue with this and setting goals that are challenging and big, is sometimes that people will stop and achieve nothing. This is often due to lack of patience, consistency and willingness to be flexible with how they reach their goals. It often means when people don't feel like they are achieving, they get up to some dodgy stuff such as:

- Start the self-worth programming comparing themselves to others, which is outright destructive

- Give up and beat themselves up for giving up

- Blame themselves, others, and the world, and then beat themselves up.

This is not why you set goals. You set goals to keep you focused and on a path. When I was teaching this to one of my student, Denisa, she asked a very interesting question. "Elliot, aren't goals very masculine?" Denisa is a beautifully feminine woman. I replied, "Yes, they are, but it's OK to have a masculine force in your life." I carried on, "If you struggle with goals, think of them as areas of focus and steps to get you there." She liked that, and that is what she uses now. I recommend that you pledge to be honest, congruent and ecological when you set your goals and are in the action.

Goals are important because they give you a reference point and a point of measurement. Traditionally, people stop at the goal setting, but in our example, it is only step one. Under the Empowering Coaching System, goal setting has four different parts:

1. Set the goals in two different ways, which will be explained further down.

2. Milestones – markers that indicate where you are in the journey, a collection of actions which mark progress and achievement.

3. Action steps – the little bitty steps that feed into creating milestones.

4. Are you ready for the fourth step? CELEBRATE! Here is the twist: celebrate success and non-success in your journey. If you are celebrating the fact that you are in action, then you are likely to take more of it and not fear it. This doesn't mean when things don't work, you go into denial. It means you acknowledge the fact that you took action and it didn't work out. The celebration is conditional on *action*. Do NOT celebrate sitting on your ass and not doing anything. This doesn't count!

Some people don't buy into the notion of goal setting. However, in my experience, that only works to a certain degree and only gets you so far. At some point, you have to be able to measure and set targets that you aim for. In my experience, when people don't set those targets, their lives don't change much down the line. Their journey peaks and levels out very quickly, and there is no growth. Most people don't set goals because of the fear of not achieving them. One year, three years, five years from now, how will you feel if your life is largely the same? And the few changes, opportunities or progress is really more the result of others' actions and desires rather than your own. It will suck, right? That's how most people go through life.

By setting goals first, it gets you off your ass and off the seat, out of your head and into action. By setting goals, you work out the end result you want and you then work backwards from there. And yes – dare to dream big. One of the people I am currently working with, their goal is to achieve a million businesses in the next 10 years. What a cool goal.

When dreaming big, please remember this saying: "People underestimate what they can do in five years and overestimate what they can do in one year." My mentor taught me that. If it doesn't happen right away, it doesn't mean it will never happen. It simply means not now, and going back again, and again, and again, and again.

The other downside to setting goals if people don't get results right away can be that they give up or keep changing the goals and then give up. That's why you need to look at the timeline you set your goals in. Yes, they are to stretch you; you also have to be realistic. I know we create our reality; however, you also understand the level of action that needs to go into a huge goal. Most people underestimate the amount of action, hours, sweat and emotional dedication that goes into achieving goals. I certainly did, and I got fairly successful and thought I made it. Then the universe sent me a test of how much I wanted the goal and how much I loved my purpose.

On that note, my purpose is at the base of everything I do, every product I deliver and every seminar I create. This all happened because of my story. I don't live in it. I accept and acknowledge it, I am grateful for it. That doesn't mean it wasn't fraught with lots of pain, heartbreak, and challenge.

My story is also filled with success, amazing connections, and triumph. On the grand scheme of stories, I feel there are people who have greater stories who have overcome far worse events in life. On the other side, this is not a competition. When I stand on stage, I say that I have lived in a war-torn country, that I was from a generation where getting divorced was not cool and my dad was an alcoholic. I come from a family where when I was growing up, my mum spent most of her time working to pay the bills to feed us. I had a brother who couldn't communicate with me, which meant I was very lonely. I am also from a generation where being dyslexic was not a common or accepted problem; was grossly misunderstood and that wasn't an excuse.

I get some very empathetic eyes when I also add in that in one month I lost pretty much all my clients, and fell into dispute with my subcontracting clients, which meant my business was on the brink of bankruptcy, and I got dumped by the girl who I was in love with. She left me for a billionaire. How did I overcome it?

I kept going, refining, getting coaching, mentoring and masterminding solutions until I was back on the path. Guess what? We never really arrive. Growth is an endless destination. I still get coaching, mentoring and mastermind to keep heading towards my goals. In order to maintain momentum, you have to build goals that are in line with your values. That's how you drive towards your purpose and vision. Setting goals can be done in various areas of your life at different times; I would highly recommend you don't do all areas at once because you will simply create overwhelm and do nothing. The areas you can set goals in are:

- Health

- Wealth

- Relationships

- Money

- Family

- Friends

- Career

- Personal development

- Business

There are various types of goals, and they all feed into achieving your life goals. You will not achieve them all. When you aren't setting clear goals, you end up with the illusion that you are doing a lot of things, yet you are easily distracted simply because it isn't what you want. You work harder not smarter. You are running after the shiny penny: the Hollywood illusion. That's when you get sucked into fulfilling everyone else's goals. Goals keep you on target and track. They keep you focused on what you want from life. There will be challenges all along the way, but there will also be rewards. How will you create the attraction around you with your actions? How will you support the universe in the manifestation of what you want if you have no direction? And how will the universe know what to send you if you are running everywhere and nowhere? Goals indicate direction and intention, not just on paper, but also energetically, physically and spiritually. How will you achieve your dreams and visions if you don't clearly spell out the end you desire?

Let me share a story with you. Two brothers go to Thorpe Park. One brother, Paul, sits down and looks to be driven around. When that doesn't happen, he starts to wander around looking for the next best ride; he spent so much time wandering around that he barely got to enjoy all the rides he wanted to go on. His brother Ronnie, on the other hand, looked at the map of Thorpe Park days before going, worked out all the rides he wanted to go on, then researched which ones got the busiest and had the longest queues. Ronnie then designed a plan on how to get the most out of the day and achieve his goal of having the best day ever at Thorpe Park. When Ronnie got there, he set out to execute his plan. Not only did he go on all the rides he wanted to go on, he went on them numerous times because he had a plan on how to make the most of the day and achieved his goal. What's your Thorpe Park?

Another layer to goal setting is going through the *process* of goal setting. It gives you clarity on what you ultimately want. By going through the process, it will help eliminate what you don't want too. This is where knowing your values is important. There is a reason why we use the phrase "crystal clear." Give articulation to what you do or don't want. What would that be worth to you? It ensures that you are channelling and maximising your time, investing your energy and efforts into things that really matter to you and creating the life you want to live. Creating or taking your success to the next level. Goal setting makes you live more consciously and certainly helps you deal with the self-statements and the beliefs around the goals you set. By the way, Beatrix (the lady I mentioned earlier) now runs two businesses. As for me, I have been working with the same mentor for over eight years now – not only that, but when he needs me, I will jump and train for him too.

I have dedicated my whole life to learning, growing and evolving. To date, I have invested a large sum of money in my development both personally and in my business too. These are amounts that I didn't think I would invest or were needed. By investing, I now have an amount of money in my bank account that I simply never thought would be there. I have qualified in Cognitive Behaviour Hypnotherapy™ and have learnt about how our brain processes information. I want to share this with you because it will help you with the right support to understand further where and how you can step in and change your belief system, thought or images in order to support your journey to success. This section will help you understand that when you are setting goals, they are set on different levels.

Everything in this world is created on four levels:

1. **Thought** – the moment you conceive the idea.

2. **Imagination** – attaching an image to the creation in your mind.

3. **Emotion** – when you affix a feeling to it.

4. **Action** – the steps to take from mind to reality. You then attach an image to it followed by the manifestation in reality.

All these stages are equally important. Without the mental creation, there will be no physical creation. Simply by setting the goals, you already achieve 75% of the process, you see immediate success. Now all that is left is the other 25% you have set in motion, which, in other words, means taking action and allowing the forces of the universe to materialise the goal physically. A lot of people do the 75% really well lots of times. The important part to bring into reality is applying the 25% implementation, understanding that it will take time, and there will be challenges that are part of the 25%. Most people start on the journey, hit difficulty, or learn how much work is involved and stop. That's not enough, that maybe 1% of the 25%. To gain the full result, you need to fully implement the whole of the 25%. Goals are a driving force, and they drive you forward.

By now, you are starting to discover that goals represent your inner desires, passions and how impactful you will be, which in turn inspire your desires. When your goals are in line with your values, they are light and are flame lit. When you set goals that inspire, you are most connected to your source, your higher self or a higher calling. It is when your inspiration is at its peak and it lasts. Although there are challenges, you learn to embrace them.

Roll back the clock, a few years to the age of 12. It was safe to say that I was pretty wild at this point; I didn't listen at all in class and was left to my own devices. We had moved once again, my mum remarried, so there was a new man in town. My mum's husband, Norman, had a very serious accident which left me to look after him while she went out to work, pay all the bills and put food on the table. My brother also started working from a very early age so he was never around; my dad was well into his alcoholic career and wasn't really there either.

There I was, a 12-year-old carer with a man at the time I

didn't even really like. I had to deal with his pain and mood swings amongst my own mood swings, starting to be a teenager, liking girls, not being very popular and feeling lonely. I did have some friends and some very good ones who were also from broken homes. We did some pretty crazy stuff; smoking cigarettes was one of the things we did together. Every Friday, we would meet up and use what little spending money we had to buy cigarettes. Every Friday, it was like a little ritual. We would meet in the local square, put all our money in together and buy around three to four different packets of cigarettes. In a state of excitement, we would go to the local park, sit around the swings and spark up. We felt like men, and we felt like the coolest kids on the block. That place was a regular meet up for other kids on the block too. Sometimes we smoked together, and other times we would fight each other and then smoke. It really did depend on what mood we were all in. That's where I got my arm slashed with a knife by a guy who attempted to stab me and ended up slashing me instead. But not before I'd also slashed him back. I take no pride in any of those incidents or the amount of fights I got into. I learnt very quickly how anything could be turned into a weapon and how easy it was to use. If only I had used this skill when I was 12, I might not have been raped!

That day was a day I buried for years. In fact, it wasn't until I was at university that I pulled that day out of my deep memory bank. I knew then I had to deal with it, unlock myself and for it not to hold me back any longer. I knew that I was connecting and letting people in and I needed to address it.

It was triggered by a silly little incident when I was working in a very established burger restaurant in London. I was doing the late shift there, and the two managers and I were having a manly laugh. Then one of the managers reached out and grabbed my penis asking, "What's the matter, you lost your dick?" At that very moment, I laughed it off. But for the rest of the evening, I was uncomfortable, tense and kept feeling as if someone was watching me the whole time. I went home that night feeling very angry and ashamed. The next day, I woke up in a rage. I was angry at the world, I was angry with the manager, and I was very angry with myself. How could I let this happen to me again? What an idiot! I was gripping my teeth together so tightly that my mouth hurt for two weeks afterwards. I remember looking so angry that people moved out of my way when I glanced at them; if looks could kill, I would have taken out half of North London. I knew that I couldn't let the guy get away with it. Very quickly, I called up head office and got an appointment to state my case. In fairness, they were very good and moved me to another bigger branch down the road. That manager had opened a box that I didn't want opening, yet needed addressing. The same day of the incident, I went home to tell my mum and her husband. That was the first time I spoke about it openly to anyone. It was the first time I had revisited that day.

That fateful day started pretty normally: I went to school as normal, got home and checked on my mum's husband who that day appeared better than normal. I double-checked if he was OK for me to go out for a while. He said, "Yes," and off I went. I was wearing blue shorts and a string vest, which was really cool back then. (Was it ever? We will never know). I had my little asthma inhaler tucked into the top of my shorts as I didn't have any pockets. The top of the inhaler was poking out, something I didn't think to be important till later on. I remember crossing the road and this guy was standing there. As I walked across, he looked at me and said, "You have asthma right? I know this because I am a doctor." I was amazed: wow how did he know? So we ended up having a little conversation, and he started telling me that he had sex every night with lots of women and how it was like air to him.

I was completely in awe of him, thinking to myself that he was so cool. He dressed cool, he looked really good, and he was so nice. He was also giving me attention, something I didn't get at the time. He then pulled me in with the killer hook. "Do you want me to get you laid?" I was 12, lonely and full of hormones. At that moment, my heart rate shot up; I started to picture myself with women. My answer, of course, was, "YES!" He asked very directly, "How big is your penis?" I didn't know how to answer that. Then he said, "Follow me, I have a way of finding out." It didn't even cross my mind what was going to happen next. I followed with excitement, thinking I was going to see a naked woman or even get laid. He led me into an alley, which at that point didn't bother me. "Just up here," he said and led me into an abandoned flat and room. There was no woman there, just him and me. He then said: "I have a

knife in my pocket, do as I say and we will get you laid."
He dropped to his knees, pulled down my blue shorts and
started kissing me there … I remember being pushed up
against a wall while he was doing that. All I could think
about was not getting hard because I didn't like it. I
remember repeating it to myself what felt like hundreds of
times. I thank God I didn't! After a while in frustration, he
turned me around in an attempt to take things to the next
level. I don't how or why, but I simply said, "My mum will
be looking for me around here." He stopped and told me,
"You are a medium size. See you on the corner tomorrow
at four p.m. and we will get you laid," and he promptly ran
out of the door. I pulled up my pants and walked home.

I remember getting home, having a bath and really
scrubbing myself, and here is the weird part. Once I was
clean, I took a whole bottle of aftershave, poured it on my
penis as a disinfectant and it burned like hell. I put clean
clothes on and went to bed for the night. Strangely, I knew
what he had done, and I knew it was wrong! Yet, the next
day, I went back to the spot where we met to see if he
would meet me for me to get laid. Just in case, I borrowed
my friend's bike, rode to the spot and waited. A part of me
wanted him to show, the other part of me felt sick. I waited
for five minutes and rode off. As I was riding, I felt dirty,
angry and ashamed.

For the next few days I was quiet, which was unusual for
me. I went quiet because I was locking away what
happened and I never thought about it again till that day
when the manager reached out and grabbed my penis. After

a few months of denying and fighting what was coming up for me, I decided enough was enough and I had to face the event. I was 19 when I decided to do that. Often I get asked why I openly discuss this. I discuss this because I want you to understand that regardless of your past and the pain you might have experienced, and regardless of what obstacles that might have been in your way, your past does not define you. Your past outcomes do not define you, neither do your past failures. What has happened has happened. This is about you taking charge of your own destiny and creating the future you want.

The guidance of a coach is very important because a coach gives you the tools to deal with the challenge, tools you might not be aware of. I teach at my training and do it myself. Here is a tool for you to experience right now. If I ever experience moments where I am short of inspiration, I look inside and address whatever blockages are surfacing and the bigger picture.

I apply the 3 A's:

- Accept.

- Acknowledge.

- Ask.

I ask myself, "Who am I doing this for?" This is a key question for me; I was laying there in Acton, wondering how I was going to pay rent and get myself out this mess I was in, this was the question I kept asking myself. Ask yourself this question now: who are you doing it for? What is your answer?

The answer for me is always for the greater good. This reminds me of what's really important to me and then I get over it. When you are in line and focused, your brain will look to create solutions to get what you want. That's when your energy and balance are restored. However, give yourself the space to let this happen, don't fight it!

By becoming a living example of an action taker and setting goals it creates laser focus in your journey. When you have become an action machine, then you can let go of goal setting. However, to begin with you need direction and focus, and laser focus at that.

1. The first step is always to accept your current situation and that you want to do something differently.

2. Agree on what is the outcome you want to create and what is the way forward.

3. Set goals to get you moving forwards and make sure they are aligned to your values and your purpose.

If you type into a satnav a town destination, sure it will get you to that town; however, will it get you specifically where you need to go? Seems simple doesn't it? Remember when goal setting that unless you are specific with laser sharp focus, you will end up somewhere nearby but not exactly where you want to be.

Strategy

Take a second to write down what your definition of strategy is?

_____

_____

_____   _____

According to the *Oxford Dictionary* website it is: "A plan of action designed to achieve a long-term or overall aim: time to develop a coherent economic strategy." I want to be very clear. Goals are not a strategy; strategy is the sexy steps that direct you towards your goals. Strategy is the plan, yes plan, of how you are going to achieve your goals that include your action steps, timelines and execution points. Goals give you a single focal point for your attention. Goals are part of your strategy. People often mistake the two and simply set more goals instead of refining the strategy. I realised that so many people make this mistake that I launched a second company called Strategic Brilliance Services to educate people on strategy and its importance. Remember goals tie into your purpose! Purpose is why you set goals to begin with. Your overall purpose gives you a broad, directional focus. Different goals for different areas in life.

I often get people telling me they don't know what their

purpose is, which is why it is also the first piece I cover when I do my strategy days. There are five simple questions you can use, which you will see in a moment. Remember to be honest with your answers and let them flow; just write your answers. The chances are you might have been asked this before; if you have, let's revisit; if you haven't, just answer honestly. Before you proceed, be very specific with your answers. Don't simply say, "I am passionate about helping people," or "I am passionate about passive income." These are Hollywood answers! Be real with YOUR answers. Some past answers have been:

"I am passionate about supporting young people between 12 to 14 years old to overcome social anxiety."

"I am passionate about getting a strategy on the page to 10 million businesses."

"I am passionate about getting people into Rwanda to embrace entrepreneurship."

"I am passionate to work with people to help and support them over inner conflicts leading to a more peaceful world and effective ways to deal with disagreements." That's my one.

Be very specific when answering, and it might take you a fair few times before you get it right.

1. What are you 100% passionate about that you will have time, physical space, money and energy for?

_____

_____

_____

____

2. Where can I add value (don't worry about how), what problem can I help solve?

_____

_____

_____

____

3. What can I bring to the table? Skills, Knowledge, Contacts, Time?

_____

_____

_____

____

4. What will it give my lifestyle, my legacy and me, and how will it be funded?

_____

_____

_____

____

5. What lifestyle will it give me?

_____

_____

_____

____

Remember, you want clear direction of what it is you want to achieve. By creating different goals for different areas, it will give you laser focus on what exactly to spend your time and energy on, as well as when to spend it. Here is the key:

Learning you can have everything you want, but not all at once.

Allow the time for things to grow and take their course. One of the downsides of people setting goals is that they don't want to wait for the results and are quick to give up. Everything needs time, and different aspects need different periods of time. This applies to achieving results.

Here is another downside. When you don't have goals, how will you know when you are there? Sure you can sit and wait for Lady Luck, for that knock on the door saying, "You have been spotted for the latest hit movie, so pack your bags and move to Hollywood." Maybe you would flip the page where I reveal the winning formula to guessing the lottery numbers every time. By not setting any goals, you are simply floating, drifting and aren't in control. You will be watching other people, feeling that success happens to other people. That other people can do it better than you.

Another downside is that you will be pulled from one bad decision to another. You will be chasing the dream while others will be creating the dream. Your energy will be so spread that you will often feel burnt out, tired and fed up. You will be attracted to hype and partake in activities that play no role in the larger scope of your success. However, you wouldn't be aware of it on a conscious level and to you this might even be normal. You are not aware of it because you are just living life as it is. You end up taking on and partaking in things that feel nice and make you feel good such as:

- Lots and lots of meetings with lots of people and doing nothing.

- Continuous learning without actually putting it into action.

- Going to lots of seminars, having lots of breakthroughs and going back to your everyday life.

- Following EVERY idea that comes to mind with false hope that this is "the one".

What happens is you end up labelling activities as important, but they are actually time-consuming. The issue is you end up distracted and not on track.

How many times have you sat with someone who told you

that they wanted to be something but life got in the way? Or they always wanted to pursue their dream but this or that happened to them? You may have a broad idea of what you want to do, and while reading this book, you might even be at a fair level of success. Until you clearly articulate specific goals, you are not directing your mind, higher self, energy and efforts properly. It's easy to get swept away by the currents of events, social media, and challenges. You may get the general overall impression that you are moving in the right direction, get a promotion and even get to a certain level of success as an entrepreneur, many do. The long-term success is just an illusion. Because how do you know you are there, got to where you want to be, and how to move forwards from there?

Goals also make you accountable. I speak about accountability in another chapter in the book, and there is reason why accountability plays a huge part in your journey. Goals create and make you accountable. They give a coach like myself something to hold over your head and remind you where you are heading.

Something rather amazing happens when you share and make a statement about your goals. By writing down your goals, you become accountable. Otherwise, it is just talk and talk is cheap. Once you write them down in the formula I share and state you are going after them, you become obligated to take action, and as your coach I will make sure you do! Believe me, if I wanted to be liked I wouldn't have chosen coaching as a profession. Being accountable means being committed to yourself; being committed to your success; being committed to do something with your passion, ideas and business; being committed to making a difference whether that would be for your family or hiring people to feed theirs.

Accountability = Commitment. Because you are willing to put yourself out there and do whatever it takes. This accountability, in essence, is accountability to yourself, your higher self and, of course, to whomever you are sharing your goals with. It's to your family, it's to your friends and it's to the universe. When you stay accountable towards your goals, you are, in fact, staying true to your desires and become an action machine.

Here is a downside to becoming an action machine that sets goals and is accountable: you will meet time and energy vampires. Energy vampires are the people who as soon as they start talking, you feel your energy and life being sucked out of you. They spend a lot of time talking about themselves. They spend time talking at you. They spend time boring the life out of you. They can also be the person who always wants to meet at the pub to talk about irrelevant topics. For some strange reason, you feel you have to please them as you don't want to be rude or a bad person. Because of them you end up falling short, getting distracted and taken in different directions. There, you have to take the necessary action to turn the situation around. If they are not supportive in your journey, then they are stopping you. Ask them politely to step aside, because you are a person on a mission.

It isn't always easy because a lot of these people are friends and family. Remember this is your life. Unsure how to check? Examine how you have been spending your time and where you are in terms of reaching your goals. Are you prioritising your tasks and action steps? Which of those tasks get you closer to your goals? Who are the people that you know will distract you or waste your time? Cut out the time wasters or activities! Once you have done what needs to be done, reward yourself with your weekly drink down the bar or weekly cup of tea with your friends. Other distractions include constantly checking your email, Facebook Twitter, etc. This is what you do when you have some downtime. For an hour a day, you do whatever you want to do. Call all your friends, go on Facebook. This is your hour to go crazy with all the time-wasting activities in the world. This is your reward for working hard towards your goals. After a while, you won't want to take your hour off, but to begin with, please do.

On this journey, you have a cut-off point. This is important if you start this journey while still having a job. If you are anything like I was, I used to run home to work on my coaching business. I would work all hours in the evening with no cut-off and then work all day. I had no downtime. Then I implemented a cut-off point, which allowed me to have my hour and downtime. I could then also switch off before going to bed. You owe it to yourself to do this. Otherwise, you burn out.

Another reason I am still in this day and age an advocate for goals is because they make you, and transform you into being, the best you can be. Remember this is not a competition. Goals help you achieve your highest potential, and they create the hunger to carry on striving for more. Without goals, you may stay in that place called "safe" and feel comfortable. The risk is that familiarity is the nemesis of growth; being comfortable slows down growth, and if you are not growing, you might as well be dying. Sound extreme to you? Watch people who have worked all their lives and got to retirement and their life didn't have meaning or focus vs. people that have worked all their lives with drive and ambition. Consider those who simply let life drift by. They start to get ill, their health deteriorates, and they have nothing to aim for. Once the buzz of being retired wears off, people start to fade away. I have watched this time and time again. Because there is nothing to aim for, no higher cause or purpose, your whole being has been about the day you retire and then you get there and are left with, "Is this it?" Not growing halts you from becoming the best person you can be. It denies you from tapping into all that potential inside you and expressing it.

Replace the word "goal" with "target" or "area of focus" for a second. Set targets to strive for and to measure progress. These targets will enable you to venture into new places, new opportunities, new highs and lows, new types of pressure and rewards, new contexts, new situations. That is where growth lives. These targets stretch you beyond your normal self. Now replace targets with goals. I have gone for various goals in my journey. With some I succeeded and some I didn't. Some I got right away and some took much longer than I planned. For example:

- I had a goal to make 100K in a year. It took me three years to do that.

- I had a goal to get 10 clients in a month and I did right away.

- I had a goal to make £10,000 in a month to go to Australia, and I did that.

- I had a goal to speak in four countries in a year, it took me two years to do it.

- I had a goal to raise three million pounds before I had a business, yep, didn't happen.

When I have gone for goals regardless of the outcome, I have found myself constantly uncovering more potential, which I did not know existed before, stretching the boundaries further and further. Let's take Eve. Eve now runs East Meets West Club. However, it has been a long journey of trials and is ongoing. Eve came to me a closed, tough woman. Her first sentence to me was, "I want to be a rich bitch." What a lovely introduction. "Are you ready to do the work to become rich and maybe not be a bitch?" She nodded her head. Great. Through the year on the advanced training, we looked at what it was she wanted to create. We set goals around launching it, getting it started and agreed to be open to learning the lessons. You see, Eve doesn't have a lot of patience. Do you know anyone like that – everything has to happen now? Building a business doesn't work like that, and if you hear anyone tell you they can make you a millionaire in a year, fucking run. If anyone says that you need them, run as quickly as you can in the other direction. Back to Eve. We set goals for the numbers she wanted in the room and the amount of members. Within the first year, she got 1,000 members to her East Meets West Club, and she has now launched a VIP level. Each time something did or didn't work out, we learnt how much fight she had in her and how much she wanted it. We discovered how to do something differently and better. If you said to me that I would be able to make £36,000 in a weekend three years ago, it would have been met with, "Yeah right." If you said to me that I could grow my seminars by a third within six months, I would have looked confused. By setting these goals, we reached them and more.

Each goal will come with its own set of challenges and rewards. Without them, I wouldn't have taken the path of least resistance and would have been another has-been in a world full of wannabe's. Goals have been instrumental in my growth, the growth of my clients and getting success to be part of my daily agenda. They have made me face and overcome countless barriers, made me more self-aware and created an undying desire to learn more and more. To improve every day and face the person I see daily in the mirror. Now I like the person I see because hand on heart I can say, "I do that! I made it happen." Can you? That is why I am still an advocate of goals.

How to set goals

I am going to introduce you to two goal-setting methods. One method works the left side of the brain and the other method will work the right side of the brain. The right side being your creative side and the left brain being your factual side. What we want is a balanced approach to setting goals with an intellectual approach and buy-in mixed with an emotional buy-in. That way we engage your whole brain.

Here is a very simple way of goal setting:

Insert the date, and always go with the first date that comes to mind because our subconscious knows.

"It is _____ date.

"I am/ I have ... (fill in what you have achieved, written on the day you achieved it or looking back as if you achieved previously) ...

End step/ How do you know? – What is the physical proof that you have achieved your goal?

Then you fill in at least five action steps that will get you there

Action Steps:

    1.

    2.

3.

4.

5.

For Example:

It is the 7th of July, I am standing in my new office having raised funding. I know this because I am holding the keys for the door in my hand.

5 Action Steps:

1. Finish business plan by the 5th of April.

2. Submit for review on the 6th of April.

3. Arrange investment pitch by 20th of April.

4. Review contracts 29th of April.

5. Sign lease 1st of May

Or something a bit more personal:

It is the 4th of September 2015, and I have been promoted at my job, and I know this because I am holding my new contract and I start on Monday.

5 Action Steps:

1. Decide what area I want promotion in, research the job and what it entails while exploring external options, to be done by the 3rd of April.

2. Discuss promotion with the manager, to be done on the 6th of April.

3. Ask for extra assignments. Put in at least 15 hours of overtime for a month starting on 10th of April.

4. Attend at least four external interviews by 15th of July.

5. Decide on the best option forward after discussing the promotion with the manager, having at least one offer on the table by 31st of July.

Always place goals in the 'now' and act as if you have just achieved them. As if each goal has already happened, and then everything around you will start stretching that elastic band to make it from today to when you want to achieve your goal. By writing in the now or in the past, it also gives us ownership over the goal. What most people tend to do is write in the future: in three months I will be, in six months, etc. Now that type of goal setting has its place when you run a business and need to plan ahead. Then you have a plan to execute the goals. For personal goals, it is no good because you are placing it in the future and you have no ownership around it and it feels distant from you; therefore, you are unlikely to keep going. Writing in the now or the past gives you immediacy and also programs your belief filters to keep going and seeking the success of the goal. You can use this formula for long-term or short-term goals, even to set daily goals. Read long-term goals out loud every day for at least 21 days.

Here is the second part: next to each goal you do a CDAR analysis of the goal.

Once you have written your goals out, you then do the CDAR assessment for each goal:

Currently – What is your current situation in regards to the goals set? Write everything down that relates to the goal.

Dilemma – This is where you get to do a brain dump, you simply write down all your thoughts around the situation. Why it has to happen and what would be the benefits. Why it hasn't happened, what are you afraid of by going for this goal; what would be the rewards if you did. You just dump everything that is going on in your head on a piece of paper. This isn't to be read back or a masterpiece, it is simply your thoughts on a page in regards to the situation around the goal set. By doing this, it will help clear a lot of the crap around the goal.

Actions – Once you have dumped all your dilemmas, you are now clear to write all the actions that you need to take to achieve the goal; what are the small action steps you need to take? List them. A good way to know if the actions you are writing down are any good is to look at the dilemmas. Do they counter or empower the thoughts you had to achieve the goals? Are the actions you are listing going to get you to achieve the goal? If there is a mismatch, keep going back and changing the actions until the action empowers you and counters any fears you might have.

Results – You also think forward about the results you want when taking those actions. This also helps to make sure you are on the right track. Thinking of the results upfront will also challenge you to see that everything is in line with what you want to achieve.

The CDAR method is designed to capture the logical side of the brain while the first method engages the right side of the brain. The more we can engage both sides, the more likely you are to keep going and achieve the results you want. This method, once mastered, can take a few minutes, but it will take a while at the beginning.

When do you think would be a good time to start? NOW!

How To Make Judgement Your Friend

Here is an interesting thing. This might read as a little strange: I remember being really small and in hospital; laying there with my arms raw, red and bleeding, the nurse cutting up cotton wool, dipping it in warm water. Then placing it over my raw arms to clean them up. Apparently this happened when I was under one year old.

I was with pretty bad asthma, eczema and allergies. From the moment I was born, I was gasping for air. From that day, I lay there with warm cotton buds on my arms and I knew deep down inside of me that I was different. I don't know how, I just did. That was one of the very first beliefs I formed.

Besides my frequent visits to hospitals with asthma attacks, I can't remember much about my first six years, except my learning about new allergies, a couple of nannies and the layout of the house where we lived in Hendon. My childhood was pretty uneventful. Just as you think everything is plain sailing and life appears to be normal, life has a way of giving you a surprise.

The big change happened when one day I came home and both my parents told me that we were moving to Israel. Ever stop and wonder what life would have been like if only things worked out differently? I don't, it's a waste of time. Off we went. I knew that we were Jewish, but besides that, I didn't really have an understanding of what it meant. Moving to Israel seemed just like moving to another house with a plane ride in between.

Talk about a change of culture. The class went from being 20 to 40. Everything seemed a lot louder and aggressive, very aggressive. Besides lots of kiddie-type arguments, a fair few fights, a ruler being broken over my head, and being made fun of because of eczema, asthma and being English and not being able to read or write in Hebrew, or English because of dyslexia, it was pretty uneventful.

One event, however, does stick in my mind: by the time I was nine we had moved four times. I got home and my mum and dad sat me down and said, " We need to talk to you." Now, by this time I learnt that acting out got me some attention, getting injured was a regular occurrence as was having asthma attacks. I also learnt to take a few things without permission, normally money. Throughout my nine years on earth, my relationship with my dad wasn't a great one. He clearly favoured my brother and didn't really have patience for a kid who was ill all the time. He didn't know how to communicate or speak to me. When he did, it was often to shout at me or give me a good old smack to stop me from doing something. I am not saying I was the easiest kid in the world, but a hug every now and then wouldn't have gone amiss.

There is never a wrong action, you can only ever react with the resources and knowledge you have at the time. For example, I remember when I was four and I was doing my normal thing of scratching the backs of legs to the point they were bleeding a lot. I called for him to come up and rub some cream on my legs, which helped me stop itching and treat the skin. I remember him opening the door, taking one look at my legs and smacking me one just above where I was scratching. This was followed by the question, "Why did you do that?" Hmmm, let's think about it for a second. I am four years old with eczema, my skin is itching, and I am not yet fully trained in mind control or coaching techniques. I was probably not aware that maybe on some deep level I was crying out for help or maybe a hug. I did what every four-year-old did when his skin was itching, I scratched. You don't know what you don't know. You can only react or do with the resources that you have at the time.

That incident really did sum up our relationship up until our conversation that evening when I was nine. I would do something, no one would really understand why, neither would I. I did it, and I would get into trouble. When I came home that evening to be told that mum and dad were getting a divorce, I didn't know what to feel or think. All I felt was another thing was wrong with me and in some way it was my fault. I saw the positive side of it. I would have two homes to go to and would pick which one I would stay at.

Something inside told me not to tell people, and I didn't. It certainly wasn't the norm in Israel. A year went by, and we had moved flats again, and it was one afternoon walking back from playing that I let slip that my parents were divorced. I remember the look on my companion's face. His eyes dropped, and he put his arm around me and told me how sorry he was. He then stopped to call on a friend and told me to go home, which I did. The next day when I got to school I might as well have had "freak weirdo" written on my forehead. The class had changed towards me. I got attention from girls, something that I hadn't had before, some people stopped talking to me and others just didn't know what to do or say. All this from telling people that my parents were divorced! That was one of my many encounters with external judgement and the power of a sympathetic story.

I wasn't the best dresser because we didn't really buy new clothes very often, and we didn't have a lot of money either. Therefore, I felt very isolated; all in all, I was a nice kid, and really I was. However, I didn't have much of an ability to express myself in a productive way. Therefore, my social skills weren't perceived as great. Adding to that I didn't have a great deal of good looks or coolness, it led me to feel very different and on my own a lot of the time. Idle thumbs make for the Devil's work, which is why I found myself in lots of trouble. Because the only way I felt I would get noticed was to go against others, especially the teachers, because the other kids would find it funny too. At least I was funny at the time. I had this inner belief: I wasn't like the other children who appeared to have everything. Which, of course, now I know wasn't the case, but the little boy in me felt that for years to come.

From then on and for the next three years – between 12 and 15 – I was pretty rebellious, I under-achieved in school, and started to hang around with an interesting crowd. I took up judo for a couple of years and seemed to do OK. I competed a few times, and even came third once. I wouldn't miss a session. I remember when I asked to join another club because the teacher saw potential in me, which, by the way, was a line I got from everyone whenever I did anything. I remember visiting the club. Everyone seemed meaner and bigger than me, a bit like the moment when Daniel from the original *Karate Kid* walked into the enemies' club for the first time. That's how it felt to me. I had a few words with the teacher, and he invited me to attend their next training session. I accepted. I was thrown everywhere and on my ass a lot. It made me angry and determined. I made the only decision a young boy can make when he has his ass kicked. I joined that club. They were faster and meaner, and I had to adapt quickly, which I did. Within six months, I was throwing guys twice my size and beating everyone in the club. When you get focused and have a reason to change, change can happen quickly. Part of that is upping your standards, effort and aim.

Sadly, there is no glory beyond that. I represented the club a few times when we travelled to fight other clubs. Then came the time for me to step up and start training for a brown belt that was way beyond my age. It wasn't only judo that kept my attention, I also devoted some of my time to Roller Skating Dance; yep, every Friday I would do that, and in a very similar fashion I attracted attention from the national squad and was offered a place with the elite skaters who toured internationally. Inside of me was a deeply embedded mismatch. My results were way outstripping my confidence or self-belief. After all, I was getting attention for good reasons, and I didn't know how to handle it.

I ended up walking away from both clubs, spending more time on the streets, coming back very late and arguing with my mum a lot. She would wait almost nightly, as I came home late. I would tell her that I was old enough to take care of myself and not to worry. I started stealing from shops and selling the goods, smoking was more than just a weekend thing, and I was fighting.

My mum, seeing this and the guys I was hanging out with, made a bold decision. She decided instead of seeing me turn into a criminal, we would move. I hated her for it, and the place we moved to, yet this would turn out to be one of the best things she ever did. We moved to a much smaller town, a bit like *Cheers* where everybody knows your name. I joined the school there and started afresh. For some reason people liked me. I was funny. The first day there started with a big opening ceremony to welcome the New Year. The place felt so big, and there were so many students. My first act of getting noticed was to drop my Walkman in front of everyone and get laughed at. It took a few weeks for me to truly warm to people and let them in.

For the first few weeks, I was quite withdrawn and I actually behaved. At home, something different started to happen. When I stopped crying and telling her that I wanted to go back and started to adapt, my mum and I started actually talking to each other, not shouting (there was still a lot of that to come), we started communicating. That was the beginning of our friendship. We talked in a way we had never done before. I started to show her a little bit more respect, mainly because I was also more dependent on her, and we had to drive to lots of places.

The people in the area were different. I still found my way to hang around with the troublemakers, and I still was every teacher's nightmare. Some teachers used to walk in, look at me and say, "Do you want to leave now, or do you want to wait till I throw you out?" I would get up and leave, go ride my friends' motorbikes, take a walk to the stables nearby, ride on the horses or walk around and find who else had been thrown out.

My ambition level was very low, and my biggest aspiration was to drive a big semi-trailer. That's all I wanted to do. I felt like I was pretty doomed career-wise, I used to come home at the end of term and count how many subjects I failed. Yet everyone told me that I had so much potential if only I would focus and listen. Famous last words. My reputation was a mixed one between being a cool kid, a wild one and a fighter. I knew a lot of very dangerous people who thought I was cool, and if I ever needed anything, all I would have to do was call them. I didn't very often if ever. You will see that because of my high judgement of myself, it lowered my ambitions because then I couldn't fail, and I found myself mixing with the wrong people. You might have been in a similar situation in your journey so far, maybe you are in it right now?

By this stage in my life, both my dad and my brother had gone back to live in England. My dad wasn't being much of a dad. My brother and I still didn't really talk, therefore, it didn't make a difference where I was. One day, I was sitting on the living room sofa and mum took a call. All I could hear was, "I told you, you should have done this years ago," and she hung up. She turned to me and said, Elliot, your dad is an alcoholic and has now gone into treatment. My heart sank even more; I was angrier than I had ever been with him. That was it; I wasn't interested in anything he had to say, and in my mind I had NO dad so I would tell people he was dead, to me. He did attempt to write, but I wasn't interested. I had a new family now, my friends. I learnt all about loyalty from those guys, what brotherhood was really about and what belonging to a community was really like. I was still a pain in the ass, but

I was a more likeable one.

One of my favourite pastimes was climbing on top of the roof where we had the hot water boiler and sitting there looking out to the sea; I would stay there for hours. That is also where I kept my cigarettes. Smoking or not, I would sit there for literally hours, fascinated by the calmness I felt while gazing out to the sea, by the different colours and the reflection of the sun on the water. I would lose myself for hours. My friends knew that if I were at home and didn't answer my phone, they would find me on the roof. Often, they would jump up and join me there for a chat and smoke. That's where I would go to gather my thoughts, compose myself and find peace.

It was that same place where I climbed up to watch one of the missiles, which was fired into Israel during the first Gulf war. In hindsight that could have been a stupid move had it had chemical weapons in it. We knew that where we were staying was so small and off the map that we weren't at risk. Still, sitting in a sealed room wearing gas masks until we were told otherwise, was not a nice experience.

Besides our negative attachment to our story, one of the key barriers when we want to strive towards success is the pain we carry around as a result of it and the amount of suffering we choose to feel. This is what we call JUDGEMENT: The word that has so much negative connotation. Judgement night, judgement day, being judged, "Are you judging me?", "The judge will give the verdict."

Whether we like it or not – and most of us don't like judgement – it is a huge driver of our behaviour. From all my years of working with clients and in my model of the world the fear of judgement is one of the biggest barriers to taking action, making a change or letting off something that is haunting you from the past.

Right now, think of yourself in front of 1000 people delivering a speech or quitting your job to truly follow your passion, which is against what you have always done or are expected to do. Now imagine that you have fallen in love with a Catholic if you are a Protestant, that you have fallen in love with a Muslim as a Jew. Now think that you came last in the race again or that your partner is right and you are wrong again. Do you love to be wrong? What are the feelings you associate with getting it wrong? Can these questions show you how much judgement plays and will play a part in your journey all the way? There would be one dominating emotion around all those questions: judgement. Judgement is an emotion driven by ego and is layered with various other emotions and needs. One of judgement's biggest emotions is fear: fear of not being accepted and fear of looking like a fool. Then throw in resentment, sarcasm, and anger. There you have it: you have the make up of judgement.

Judgement is nothing more than perception, your perception of yourself, your perception of others and their perception of you. Is there any wonder we hate judgement so much? There are two main types of judgement: external and internal. Guess which one came first? External.

External judgement

External judgement has been with you all the way. Since the moment you were born, you were judged. Think about it for a second: When you were born the words: "Isn't he/she beautiful?" "Doesn't she/he look divine?" At this point, you have not even farted for the first time and you have been judged. If you were really unlucky you could have been judged the opposite, "Why, that's an ugly baby" or "That's a big baby," and those were the first words your beautiful self heard even if you have no memory of it. Then you started to grow up and went through the years of being very cute and sweet and smelled great too, between nappy changes. All the judgement that was coming your way was mainly positive, except when you wanted something; you couldn't speak, your parents couldn't understand you, it all got very frustrating. As you kept growing, you started to explore. You started to touch things, taste things and formulate sounds that would sound like words. Then you carried on and started to speak a little, respond to questions and even ask for things a little. At this point, you were still very much getting positive reinforcement. Then came the day: judgement day. The day you were asked to do something, pick something up and you said, "NO!" Then one of your parents said, "What did you just say?" and you responded with, "No, I don't want to!" At that moment you weren't being the best baby in the world, the cutest baby in the world and the image of excellence has gone out of the window for your parents. "You will do as I say or else," and welcome to external judgement. Suddenly these big people that you had been playing with stopped being nice and you didn't know why. Or did you understand why? All you did was say, "no." If they didn't want you to use that word, why did you hear it so much? Then you start to hear phrases like, "be a good boy/girl and do this ..." or "Are you going to do what I say or are you going to be a bad boy/girl?"

This is when you start to hear "good boy/girl", "bad", "naughty", "I told you NO!" "You silly boy/girl" ... and welcome to being defined by judgement. You also have your parents secretly telling you what they want you to be. You are going to be David Beckham. My girl will marry the Prince of England, she is already a princess. All you were doing was soaking it all in. You were letting everything around you leave an imprint. This is where you learned that big people say things and what they say has a meaning, which at times you were supposed to know but didn't because no one really taught you that. You learned the hard way. You were like this big sponge just soaking it all in, forming patterns that drive your behaviour even today. You were forming neuropathic ways of what means what. What equals what? Why, how and what.

I remember when I was sitting down to have dinner when I was staying at a hotel doing some corporate work. I sat at the table and behind me were a grandfather and grandmother with a child waiting to get to their flight. The hotel was basically next to an airport up in Liverpool. I couldn't help but overhear what the granddad was saying to this young four-year-old. "If you don't eat all your food, the pilot won't be able to take off. That's why it is important that you eat everything; otherwise, we won't get you home to Mummy and Daddy. Now be a good girl and finish your food."

I thought with my coaching hat, 'Oh, wow, what pressure to put on her and she is in the formative years where everything counts. She is being told that everything depends on her.' I am well aware that the granddad didn't mean any harm. However, that is a prime example of our interactions and the language we soaked up as kids, which introduced us to our friend "judgement".

Then you learnt that certain actions equal good feedback and certain actions equal bad feedback. Not rocket science. You also learnt that reacting in certain ways got you certain reactions back. Then you learnt to play on it too. As you kept growing up so did the size of the judgement. Because you didn't know better, everything that you were told you took as truth, well most of it.

Let's rewind the clock back and do the following:

1. What were the key phrases that you heard about you while growing up? For example, "He is the clever one", "She is the quiet one", "I love you because you are good at ..."

_____

_____

_____

____

2. Did you have any nicknames? What were they?

_____

_____

_____

___

3. How was behaviour reinforced? "If you don't do your homework you won't succeed," "Good girls clean their room."

_____

_____

_____

___

4. How were you judged growing up? List all the judgements you had growing up and even till this day.

_____

_____

_____

___

5. Now comes the key question: What truth is there to any of them?

_____

_____

_____

___

Internal Judgement

You started to develop your own internal judgement and started to judge yourself according to how many times you got praised and how many times you were naughty, and when the people that we loved told us we couldn't do something, we believed it. When they said that good things don't happen to people like us, we believed them. When they said that we were to be seen and not heard, we believed them. When they said that good people succeed and naughty people don't, we believed them. What else did we have to go on? One of the most heartbreaking moments is when you see a little kid ask their parents: "Mummy and Daddy, are you happy you had me?" "Mummy and Daddy am I a good enough son or daughter?" Absolutely heartbreaking. Now, where would they pick that up from if it weren't being imprinted on them by their environment?

When you started interacting with other kids, it was a different ball game. Do you measure up to other kids? Are you liked? If you aren't, why not? What's wrong? And if you are born slightly different than others physically, it is suddenly magnified because that's what defines you, according to other people. This isn't a criticism, just an explanation why judgement plays such a big part in our journey. Then we start to model people around us who, of course, draw different responses and different reactions. School introduces you to a whole different set of judgements and then you are measured on your results. Now your results give you feedback and popularity. Your results even show how much love you might get or not as well as rewards. The one time you cracked a joke and no one laughed; that time you stood up and read out in class and everyone laughed or you struggled and didn't sound like the rest of the kids. A teacher calling you "stupid", "lazy", "useless" or "rude", which you took as truth because they knew best, right? Maybe you were great at sport, or maybe you weren't, maybe you were OK. All coming with a different level of judgement and pressure. Maybe you were the one who messed up and it cost your school the match. Maybe you were the dreamer and were told off. Maybe you were the joker. Maybe you won the match or maybe you never really did anything and were ignored or missed out? All of these actions have different types of judgements and measures of love. You carried on soaking this in and taking it in. Each time making internal decisions about what you could and couldn't do. Then proving to yourself that you were right, and each time the event happened it further cemented what was going on with you internally.

Then you started to behave according to what was expected of you by other people, and if you behaved in a way that suited the external influences, then you were rewarded, and if you didn't, you were punished. Your behaviour at school followed the same pattern. Each result defined your internal judgement of yourself, either empowering you or disempowering you.

Think of the first time you got it wrong big time. How did you talk to yourself? What did you say to yourself? How much of other people's reactions did you use to evaluate your own expectations and judge yourself and internally beat yourself up? The chances are you made some pretty serious decisions that day and every time you got it wrong. These are the decisions that still play out in your subconscious mind. The same decisions that block the next level in your life and the same way you judge yourself every day.

Rejection

Rejection is not getting a result or an answer you wanted, which means the wanting of personal validation and acceptance. According to what we perceive to be an acceptable answer or confirmation of an outcome we wished, hoped for or wanted.

Taking that notion to mind makes rejection personal. The moment we don't get the answer we want, or feel we deserve, it collapses our identity. In our mind, we have built it out to define us or give a pathway to something that will further enforce our status or take us to the next level. When we hear rejection, all that internal build up, imagery and validation collapses. All that hype that you created comes crashing down. What's the first thing that happens? All your internal judgement kicks in, all your insecurities kick in, all your destructive self-talk sounds more like self-screaming. Someone might as well punch you or kick you.

It has been said that rejection can hurt as much as a physical injury, especially in social situations. If you are carrying around so much internal judgement, it is no surprise. You must find a way to deal or change the meaning of the situation. What do you think will be the reaction? You will either shut down because of the pain or fight back and explode. In some circumstances, it leads to violence, and in some cases it leads to long-term abuse and outbursts.

When people are living in such a state of judgement and continually having their internal identity collapse, it is no surprise that people end up lashing out, developing anxiety, living stressfully, suffering from depression and anger.

Rejection is never personal!

What happens when we wrap ourselves in the fear of judgement is that we also create a fear around rejection and that in turn also lessens our ability and clarity to take action. If you are consumed with the fear of asking or the fear of not hearing the answers you want to hear, you will stop asking! You will simply not take any action at all. You can only be rejected if you allow yourself to take it on a personal level and allow someone to collapse your identity. This doesn't mean when they are saying, "No," it is a "Yes." It means that either they don't truly understand what you are asking, see the value of what you are asking or don't like you. Their answer says more about them than you. This goes back to our childhood, which we have discussed and that moment you were told, "No" and you learnt that "No" is a bad thing. We weren't taught that "No" is a chance to ask better questions. We learn that

"No" is in some way a reflection of value. The more people say "Yes" to me, the better person I am, which, of course, is bullshit. We carry this notion still around today. Rejection = judgement in most people's minds.

If you are afraid of rejection, then it will block your ambition to ask for and create the life you want to create. *Rejection is never personal.* This is a simple and powerful notion and great for you not to spiral downwards when you get rejected unless you choose to make it personal. If you think this is all fluff, well, let me tell you a little story.

I decided to test out this notion for myself and where better than on *Britain's Got Talent* in front of 4,000 people who were hungry to boo everyone and anything, from someone who sounded like the next Mariah Carey or was cute and danced on four legs. For most people, getting up in front of others and opening up is scary enough, let alone in front of Simon Cowell and two very powerful judges.

I went along to the pre-auditions very open-minded and knew that they never had a coach on their stage. I waited all day and met some cool people; I kept on practising my act, which was to have an arrow break on my throat with a talk about fear and overcoming it. The producer loved it, and we ended up chatting for an hour. Things were looking good. When I left the audition room, I was told, "she never spends so long with anyone." 'How cool,', I thought to myself. I waited for weeks before the call came and was told that I was invited to stage auditions. I jumped up and down and started to prepare and polish the act. My business partner hated the idea. I, of course, didn't listen and wanted to get on stage in order to get my message and be the first coach to win *Britain's Got Talent*. The day finally arrived: it was February 2010. I waited for hours, and I mean hours. I got there at 2 p.m. and went on stage at 11 p.m. Nevertheless, time was spent rehearsing and drilling my presentation. A lot of people liked the concept and how original it was. Things were looking good … Then I received a call and was driven to the stage.

One of the first things you notice is how loud the buzzer is when you get near the stage; the next thing is how loud the audience is. You then notice how disappointed people are when they come off stage. What happens is you get a call and they line you up on the side of the stage, mic' you up and you are away!

I ran on stage high on energy and shouted very loudly, "HELLOOOOOOO LONDON," and got a very warm reception: '*It is on,*' I thought. Then Simon Cowell asked his normal question, "What's the dream?" "To be an international motivational speaker," was my reply. Simon then said, "OK, there is a place for you in the next round if you win this audience over."

I could feel a shift in the energy in the room. I opened my mouth and with four words they were booing. I kept on going. They went quiet when I pulled out the arrow. I thought, 'I got you' and carried on speaking. They started booing again. When I put the arrow against my throat, they fell silent again. As soon as I finished the arrow break, they were all booing and words of harsh judgement were thrown at me. The act had ended.

Piers Morgan simply said, "No" and Amanda Holden told me, "This isn't a talent." ('Neither is being spotted on a blind date,' I thought. But I kept my mouth shut before I gave them the chance to make me look ridiculous). Simon told me that it wasn't a big enough act for the show. I walked off stage.

Here is the irony. As I was leaving, I opted to walk to the station instead of going back to the holding place for the auditions. As I started to walk out, the show ended and all the audience started leaving at the same time. I was dressed the same and was the second to last act. They saw and knew who I was. I must admit that I was a little afraid, as all it would have needed was a couple of people to throw a punch because they didn't like the act. Nothing like that happened. On the contrary. As I was walking out, I heard a bunch of teenagers behind me and suddenly I heard, "You inspired me." I stopped and turned round. There were 15 teenagers gathered around me. A couple of them asked for an arrow as a souvenir; I gave them a couple of arrows and got them to promise that they wouldn't be used as weapons. I could just imagine the headlines the next day *Coach with the Hat Gives Arrows to Teenagers Who Use Them as Weapons.*" As they skipped away, one of them turned around and said, "Thank you, you've inspired me." I will never know how many people I inspired amongst the boos. However, if one approached me and she was with a group of young people, well that's 15 I inspired. What if I actually reached 5% of them, well that's 200 that I might have impacted. The truth is we never truly know our own reach and impact. I will never forget while I was a trainer for Sky TV, a lady approached and asked me: "Elliot, are you also The Coach with the Hat?" "Yes," I said. "Wow, I followed you throughout *Britain's Next Top Coach* and have followed you online too." It is the same with *Britain's Got Talent.* While it felt like 4,000 people were booing me, I might have inspired a fairly large number too.

When I decided to test this notion, I put myself out there in front of 4,000 people. I could have felt very rejected and judged by them all. I chose not to take it personally. Because I understood that it was not me they were rejecting, they were rejecting what they saw me doing. Just because I was booed, does that make me a bad person or a bad coach? Nope! During the two minutes I was on stage did they all get to know me? Did they get much about who Elliot is? What The Coach with the Hat stands for? I knew it wasn't personal. They didn't know me well enough to reject me. It is as simple as that.

Once you understand that it is never personal, rejection stops being one of your core values. It stops being one of your blocks because you are not afraid of rejection and judgement. The same goes with getting it wrong. Not wanting to be wrong or in the wrong stops you from going after things such as promotions or what we truly love; because then we start to link being wrong with rejection.

The sad fact is that a lot of people are living like this daily in their relationships with themselves, with loved ones and in business. When you are being rejected, there is a certain amount of external judgement that needs to be dealt with. Not just by the person rejecting you. Here is what happens in your mind: you then feel like you have to tell your friends, your family, or maybe people saw it happen. I believe this is a far bigger influence on feeling rejected than anything. It is the "What will people say?" internal dialogue. You know that telling people will not draw any positive internal validation. Sometimes you say nothing, sometimes you lie, or you simply tell people you don't want to talk about it and hope to bury it all. All this is very dangerous, because the pain of rejection is just like being punched in the stomach, and why would you put yourself up for pain? You don't have that problem when you have a good outcome, do you? Then you can't wait to tell the world, write it on Facebook, tweet, etc.

There is another option: you do find validation when you don't get the answer you want because people are naturally sympathetic. When you go to them and you don't get what you want, you get people that show you empathy and support you, and those are the people you would turn to. Parents are great at playing that role, close friends and, of course, girlfriends or boyfriends. Once you start to step out of that circle, the less people will give you empathy, and the more painful it is.

Because of all these ingredients, it is no surprise that judgement plays such a big part in our journey and our ability to take action. Once bitten, twice shy? Or once judged twice as judged?

Projecting Judgement

Here is another spanner in the works: the judged becomes the judge. How much do you love being judged, being talked about, being told what you don't want to hear? Yet how often do you bitch about other people? Spending your time talking about them and how they did this wrong, what is wrong with them and how they should never have done that, worn this or said that? Here is some advice: if you cannot say it to someone's face, don't say anything at all. Because one of our ways of false hoping we won't be judged is to be quick in judging other people. By judging people, we also feel better about ourselves because we are not like them, right? Because by projecting your stuff onto them you feel important and get some significance. Yet people underestimate how destructive it is from an energetic, emotional, and spiritual level.

From an energetic point of view you are expending so much internal energy on putting people down that it is toxic and also means you are operating in low vibration energetically, consequently, you will attract low energy situations and outcomes. That's why when you judge people, you find people that judge other people too because you are attracted to that level of energy. By being in that energy, what you are feeding your body isn't productive to your growth. It is heavy and draining, which will affect your state as well as your mood. You will start to filter conversation for it. It will start to eat away at you like cancer.

From an emotional point of view, it is draining, it is toxic and simply exhausting. It will tilt your moods towards anger, resentment, frustration, jealousy and stress. Once again, all low vibration states of mind and low vibration emotions, which create low vibration outcomes. Such as vindictive behaviour, victim-like attention seeking, fights, arguments and suspicion. All coming from a place of emotional scarcity i.e. always seeing what is missing. It is unbalanced and dangerous, often with a feeling of isolation and that no one understands you.

From a spiritual point of view, if you are someone of spirit that believes in the higher self, a presence of God or that we are part of a grand conspiracy of the universe, just think what you are putting out there. What are you saying to your higher self or your spiritual being? That you are too busy looking for faults in other people. You tell your higher self that you are good enough to be connected to it. You will also be blocking out the messages from your spirit because you are spending time in disempowerment and will have no room for spirit in your life. If you are someone that believes in God, what message are you sending to the Almighty?

Therefore, before you open your mouth or even internally cast your judgement on someone or yourself, beware of the many levels at which you are damaging yourself.

There is only feedback

This is one of our key teachings. There is only ever feedback. You see, when you don't get the answer you want, that's feedback. When someone said yes or no that's feedback. The more you remain detached from an answer or an outcome, the more you are able to stay in peak state. The more you are in peak state, the more you are in control. The more in control you are, the more composed you will be. However, you choose to personalise it, don't you? You choose to relate it to rejection and then all your insecurities surface unconsciously and take you back to the day you first felt rejected and the pain it caused you, and it hurts even more. You started to define yourself by the results you were getting, and if you weren't getting the answers you wanted in some way, you decided that it is a reflection of you. Often, when someone is giving you feedback, there is a chance they are giving you a little gift; of how to get what you want. A gift of what people really want to see or hear, how to improve. Sometimes, it is simply them needing to feel important, therefore offering you a piece of their mind.

I have found the best answer to this situation is simply to listen and say thank you, whatever you think; if you agree or not, like it or not. Saying thank you will defuse any tension, which is normally coming from you. It sends out a message that you have listened and are grateful for their feedback, and it also helps remain detached. I know it sounds simple and isn't always easy, yet it is so powerful when you simply say thanks for your feedback. Then you decide what to do with it.

When you adopt this peak state that there is only feedback

and nothing is personal, it opens so many doors. It keeps the door of opportunity open, the opportunity to learn and remove any thoughts of failure from your head; the opportunity to get excited. You have to approach this with balance because when you ask for feedback or take on this peak performance state it means you have to accept the negative with the positive and that people will feel even more that they can tell you stuff, normally negative. The inner strength this will give you is phenomenal. Imagine not hearing criticism, simply hearing feedback.

There is only feedback in any given situation. How liberating! No right, no wrong, only feedback. As mentioned, this does mean a lot of self-assessment on a continuous basis. It also means that continuously you have to assess your mindset to check if you are in peak state or not. The thought that there is only feedback is amazing; it also removes a lot of the pressure we place on ourselves. The quality of your life will improve. You will have less stress and fewer arguments.

Simply remember there is only feedback. You will find your ability to take action increases dramatically too and not only that, excuses will start to disappear. How liberating is that? Saying thank you and no excuses. For some people, this is completely out of their reality, simply because of their different set of beliefs; however, there is only feedback would be one attitude I would encourage you to adopt. It has changed my life. I certainly would not have dealt very well with *Britain's Got Talent* if I took it as anything besides feedback.

The reason I want to address beliefs is because they are such drivers of how we react when getting feedback. Examining where beliefs come from means considering where we grew up. The place we grew up will have a huge influence on us, our beliefs system and our association to feedback. What kind of family we grew up in, as discussed previously. Whether you grew up in a loving and warm environment or a cold one, what culture you were born into, and religion will have an influence on your beliefs and how you deal with feedback. Your schooling experiences will shape your ability and beliefs around feedback. Where you went to secondary school, high school, and college will influence your ability to deal with feedback. What happened, what was the outcome, and what was your experience around the outcome; when it worked or when you took action and it didn't work will also shape your beliefs around feedback. In most instances not getting the feedback we want or crave will make us feel disappointed, angry, resentful and hurt. This is when you learn to start hating feedback or take it as criticism. Our brains will always seek out the facts, and when you are filtering for negative ones, your mind will find the negative or whatever you have chosen to believe. Therefore, you will always find a way to justify a belief. As soon as you decide and make a choice to believe in something, your brain will always find ways to justify it. It will go on autopilot and search through your belief filters to justify what you want to create. For example, let's say you have a belief that everyone is out to trip you up on this journey. Your brain will start to filter out what doesn't support that notion and distort anything to support that notion. You will interpret what people are saying to be in line with that belief. You will affix a different meaning to people's actions and your thoughts will be dominated proving you right. This is one of the many reasons why our mind is so powerful, aside from all the other amazing functions it carries out. Our mind will always find a way.

There are two types of beliefs: positive or empowering beliefs and negative or disempowering beliefs. They live side-by-side and actually work in unison if you let them. For every empowering belief you have, you have a disempowering belief. For every belief you have around succeeding, you also have a belief that you might not. For every belief you have about winning, you also believe that you might lose. They all form your belief system. They will have huge influence on your ability to deal with feedback and how you deal with external and internal feedback. They will also influence you in terms of the action you take and how much pain you are willing to endure as part of the process. For every belief that does not serve you (and if you are slightly normal you would have a fair few of them), when you are making a decision you will be going through your belief filters, which is in turn how you justify that belief or beliefs. This happens in milliseconds. It's just as easy to create a belief that does serve you and that will support you. However, it takes time to alter the belief because you have been running on autopilot for so long. Even though you make a decision to change your belief, it needs to be done at a very deep-rooted level. Once you have changed the belief at a cellular level, the same filters will justify and empower you.

It is true, by knowing your disempowering beliefs it helps you to understand what is blocking you and where. Also, we get stronger by working on our weaknesses.

If you know what you don't want, it helps you identify what you do want.

If you know what your disempowering beliefs are, you can change them into empowering beliefs.

Beliefs are something that we can change. For you to reach the depth of beliefs and to truly be able to deal with judgement and feedback, you have to go deep.

80% has to be belief in yourself, and 20% is feedback.

I hide mine too

For years, I didn't share my story. I went through years of not even saying that I lived in Israel because of the external judgement that came with living in such a country. I went through a phase of not telling people I was Jewish because of the stereotype that goes with it. I certainly didn't tell people that I was raped. I didn't mind telling people about my dad being an alcoholic. When people asked me where I was from, I would say the UK. "You don't look English," "That's because my mum is Argentinian" "Oh, that's why," which is true, by the way. When conversation started about Israel, I would speak up yet not reveal that I lived there, and when people were slagging Israel off, I would often keep my mouth shut, why? For the simple reason that I didn't want to get involved in an argument with people who didn't want to change their point of view or got everything from the media without understanding the history.

When I talk about coming from Israel nowadays, I ask people to park the politics because then I am boxed into someone's distorted opinion regardless of what they think of the country. Here is the interesting fact – when I started to share about living in Israel and about being a dancer, people started to listen more. When I shared about my dad and my rape, people listened even more. Strange, isn't it? When I opened up, then people wanted more of me and wanted to hear what I had to say vs. hearing about my next Empowering Coaching Technique tool. Once they heard the story, they were interested to learn how I overcame it.

Your story is your greatest asset

Look back at your story, it is where a lot of your answers already lie. The difference is most people simply hang on to the pain, desperation and agony of their story. Some people go right into denial and won't ever talk about the past. Some people hang on to their story like it was still happening today and keep alive all the emotions that go with it. How many times have you met someone that keeps telling you his or her story over and over again? They are stuck in the same spot. A lot of people use it as an excuse or a reason why their life hasn't worked out.

This is what I want for you: use your story to inspire your success and inspire others. Your story is what connects you to others. It is where your wisdom, experience and knowledge lie. When I grasped this, everything shifted in my coaching and my ability to stand on stage, connect and transform people's lives. This is because people can relate far better to you when you tell your story. Something magical happens when you start to share it, something that is beyond our grasp of human understanding. Suddenly the right people show up. Suddenly you get that phone call. Suddenly you get an invite to speak somewhere. More than anything, you show people that it is OK, it is OK to talk about it.

When you share your story, you offer people hope, you show people that they are not alone. By telling your story, you are a living testimonial to the human spirit. The key to success is in our story. This doesn't mean that you don't have to go through the process of healing and dealing with the pain associated with your story. This doesn't mean that if you haven't had much pain in your journey or practically a rough time you make it up or are less important with your message. In fact, that is just as important as part of your journey. This isn't a competition. You are unique and incredible with whatever your story is and can make a huge impact.

Here is what I do when I work with people, and it comes down to their story. We do a lot of work to see how it served and what good has come of it. This is such an important step to creating detachment and to start dissolving any emotional attachment. It is also called a reframe.

For example:

- I am a failure in everything I do

- Reframe – I don't succeed in everything I do

- Reframe – there are some areas in my life I would like to be better at

- Reframe – while I have not always got it right, I will keep trying until I do

We go very deep. Every time someone gets to grips with their story, they understand its power.

This is no easy task though because it means going back and looking at it from a different angle, understanding how it has affected you and how it has played out in your life. By looking at the story and by going through all this process you are able to understand how it served you and what good it has done to you. Whenever I mention this to people, "stuff" crops up. "Are you telling me that being raped was a blessing?" "Are you telling me that losing my husband was a good thing?" "Are you telling me that being disabled is a good thing?" "Are you telling me that being bullied was a good thing?"

My response to this is, first of all, how has it served you, and then YES, what good has it done you?

The importance of this process is also to STOP you thinking like a victim, to take ownership over your story. If you are to use your story to empower people, then you must understand and truly accept how it empowered you. Imagine going to work and hearing someone speak who is still disempowered by their story, how inspiring would that be? Would that leave an impact on you?

Letting go of your story

There are some very simple steps to accepting your story and turning it into a vehicle to empower you.

- Identify your significant events, that means going back into childhood as well, and note them down.

- For each event, list all the qualities it has given you:

  o Willpower

  o Fight

  o Focus

  o Determination

  o Strength

  o Resolve

  o Drive …to name a few

- List the drawbacks that occurred as a result of these events

- List the emotions you relate to the story

- List the effect of these emotions in your life and how they show up in different situations.

Once you have the list, it is time to collapse the attachment. If you feel you might need support through the process, then I would advise doing it with a trained coach, someone that has hypnotherapy training. As these processes can be a very powerful process and need to be managed, I still do this with my clients when it is needed. The reward and freedom you will find will be worthwhile for years to come.

- Write yourself a letter forgiving yourself and read it out aloud every morning for 21 days. Here is an example of one:

  Dear

  I am writing you this letter because I want you to know that you are doing very well, and remember why you are on this journey in the first place, remember you are a gift to the world and it takes a special person to want to leave an impact in this world like you do. I want you to let go and forgive yourself, as you have done nothing wrong. I want you to trust yourself as your inner wisdom will always shine through, and I want you to let go, release this and keep moving forward. I completely love you, I trust you, and I forgive you.

Love your inner wisdom

Not Enough Money at the End of Your Month?

I run a one-day seminar all about money. This is where I work with you for a day and by the end of the day you become best friends with money. Because most of us aren't friends with money and have a very bad relationship with it. A bit like Carl's relationship with the girl: replace the girl with money. That's how most of us feel when dealing with money. Keeping in theme with our best friend connotation, money being our best friend, do you have more time at the end of the month to relax and know that everything is paid for or are you walking around feeling choked up? Do you have the time to spend with your friends and your relatives or are you chasing your tail? Your ability and where you spend your time with your best friend, money, is very much dictated by the hierarchy of your values. You see, we will always have time, space, energy and money for what is in our highest values. One can always find their best friend in their highest values. I place a high value on growth, I always found money to pay for my development, even when I didn't have £15,000. When I was turning my personal life round after going bankrupt, I knew I needed to work with a strategist. As business is one of my highest values I found my best friend was there again. You always find money for what is in our highest values.

I invested in a property which ended up leaving me

£150,000 in debt and resulted in my losing it because it was a great investment at the wrong time – because we had this little thing in 2008, you might have heard of it. I believe it is called a recession! In the end, I was in so much debt that I had to write it off.

When you attempt to go against your highest values, you will be in conflict and functioning in that dark tiresome energy. Our values drive our behaviour more than we think or understand on a conscious level, which is why at my event, *Power to Succeed*, we call them Internal Drivers of Behaviour.

Your Values are made up of what you value the most and what appears to be missing the most, and unless you have high enough value on something, it won't be in your time, energy plans or in your bank account. It certainly won't drive your behaviour to an empowering place where you have more time at the end of the month.

You are right now a reflection of your highest values and, of course, your lowest values. Take a second to look around your space, your physical space. If money is at the lower end of your values, then it will show up in that form and will be the last of your thoughts, goals and ambitions. It will be the last thing you pay attention to, and it will be hard for you to accumulate because you will be conflicted around it and busy pushing it away.

Money, like your best friend, only sticks around if it is welcome, respected and valued. There is no right or wrong, good or bad when it comes down to values, only what your values are.

There are plenty of examples of people with different values who have made a huge impact on this world and continue to do so. Even though money may not have been their highest value, they understand how it can help forward a cause, promote and open up avenues. You can do more with money than without it; you can extend your lifestyle to what you want it to be with money. Whatever the hierarchy is, you can do a lot more to serve your values and live a purposeful life with money than without. Having money will offer a life of stability as a mum or a dad.

Having money will:

- Allow you to build the lifestyle you want. Imagine waking up in the house you desire, painted in the way you want with the furniture you choose and it is done your way. It smells fresh and crisp. The temperature is just right for you. There are just the right number of rooms, and the garden is how you want it. Building the life you want in order for your family to have what they want when they want, without spoiling them.

- Allowing you to offer the gift of education of skills, spending your free time travelling to different places, maybe places you have never thought about, maybe Africa? Maybe India? Maybe it is much closer to home. Imagine all the smiley faces and people you could impact with the information you could share and transfer to the less fortunate. What if that could be your legacy? What if you could share your gift of time with others?

- It will also allow you to have the life you want, to do what you want and be the success you want to be. Recently, I experienced this for the first time, every year I go and spend Christmas with my mum out in Florida. I have created a business, which allows me to do that. I was able to go to shops and simply buy what I wanted without feeling any sort of remorse or guilt. I was able to treat myself to big nights out and still had lots of money left in my account. Now this was done in gratitude and appreciation. I would still be sensible and buy no more than I wanted. The point is I had the freedom to choose instead of being dictated to, which I had been in previous years. Money will help you do that. What would it feel like to have that kind of freedom, and you don't need millions to do that. What thoughts would you have if you could create that lifestyle? How do you think you would look?

- You could invest in your education more and keep growing

- You could save a lot more and give to various funds for different causes

This doesn't mean you have to make millions, it does mean that you have to invest time, energy and commitment to learning to do things in a different way.

There have been times in my life when I had money to invest and money in the bank. Until I dealt with my issue around my newly found best friend, I would push it, lose it or spend it. As a result until I understood the good I could do with it, and used it to empower people, it didn't stick around. Now money and I are besties, we work hard on our relationship, and we are growing. I now have clients call me up to pay early. I also have different revenue streams of income, which helps me store cash reserves. Our relationship has a way to go, but we are truly embedded in each other's lives. I treat money differently, I respect and work on our relationship. Every day I say, "All of God's wealth flows to me." A Rabbi taught me that and everyday I am grateful for whatever I have. I also celebrate every time I get paid and money comes in. Like any relationship, it comes with challenges and will drive my behaviour when it is not around because I still feel the pain of when I had none.

Want to know your attitude to money? Follow my exercise below:

I looked at money on four different levels and addressed the blockages around them:

Emotionally – What are my emotions around money? Empowering and disempowering. What actions do I take to gain it? What action do I take to push it away?

Spiritually – How can money help me on the spiritual path? How can it block me on my spiritual path?

Energetically – How can money help my flow? How can money block my flow? Where am I investing my energy in order to get my empowering results? Where am I investing the time that is blocking my energy flow?

Physically – What action am I taking that generates money and impacts me for the better? What actions am I taking that sabotage my keeping money and reinvesting? Where can I create the biggest action that will have the biggest impact?

Stop and take some time to answer these questions, it will give you some real insight into your relationship with money, then carry on.

The answers to these questions give you a balanced point of view of your approach towards money and understanding both what is working for you and what isn't. Park all your self-judgement, there are no right or wrong answers to these questions, only the truth for you.

Our conflict with money comes from a mismatch in our realities vs. expectations + experiences. I have discussed our programming around money, and this is what happens. We have an expectation around what money is meant to do for us and how it is meant to show up in our lives, most expect it will just knock on their door. Then what happens is our experience around it is normally either disempowering or negative; there is a huge mismatch and we are conflicted. Let's take one of my clients. Nami is simply one of the nicest guys you can meet, he comes from an absolute place of service. Nami came to me with over 32 years of experience in business. He built properties in Spain and sold them. He had made millions in property sales. He had lots of money, but it was running out because he hadn't done anything for a few years. He came to me very conflicted because all his life he had done very well with money but now it wasn't sticking around. Now he had to change his attitude because he had started charging people for his services, and at this point he didn't value his own expertise and knowledge. Therefore, he found it hard to ask his potential clients for money for his services. Guess who was losing out? Guess who was the one investing lots of time with no money coming the other way. You see, Nami had an expectation that money would flow to him as it did in the past. The reality was until he started to value his services, money wasn't going to come and stick around. You see, Nami wasn't friends with money. Nami expected money to show up on his doorstep, and when it didn't, he was angry and frustrated. He was conflicted with his desire to help vs. the need to charge, do you know anyone like that? Since working with us, he has overcome a lot of his issues around money. He has built up *Malaga Business Minds* and is the go-to coach in the south of Spain.

This conflict is so strong that it will take us if we let it, it will play out and you will self-destruct and ruin your relationship with your potential best friend. That's why doing the exercise above is an ongoing activity, you have to do it on a regular basis and every time you feel, sense or know there is a blockage. Like going to the gym, it takes time and practice to maintain and keep everything flowing. Just like anything in life, when you master one level, it's time to go to the next level, and that means addressing any new blockages that might be occurring. Do you really want to miss out on the best friendship you can have, which will yield the life you want and the way you want it, to do great things and impact this world, your community and your purpose in life?

Inner conflicts

A lot of people ask me where inner conflict comes from. There have been a lot of studies and research done to answer that question. I have done my own studies and research. I spent two years interviewing entrepreneurs, have worked with 100s of people internationally and studied some of the great scholars and coaches to find an answer to this question. Is there one correct answer? No. However, let me give you mine.

Inner conflict comes from:

A mismatch between expectation + experience + outcomes + beliefs & values = conflict

When we were growing up, we went through the imprint years and soaked in everything around us. We learnt very quickly what is right or wrong in our parents' model of the world; we started to make it our own model of the world.

While we are kids we are told stories and fairy tales, which always have a happy ending. At that age, it conditions us to think and see that everything has a happy ending, except while growing up we seldom do. While we are learning the ways of the world and how everything is beautiful, our realities don't match. We, therefore, develop an expectation of how things are supposed to be or how things are not meant to be.

Just think of the first time you had an amazing experience going somewhere, like a theme park. From the moment you bought your ticket, queued to get it and went in. You heard the music, smelt the food and saw all the rides in front of you. You got this feeling in your stomach. You carefully looked at each ride and started to plan your way around the park. You went on each ride, some you liked more than others, and then the day came to an end. Did you want to go home? Once the day is over you have created an expectation around the event and had an experience. The next time you go back, you will have an expectation. All it takes is one slight change and it affects our whole experience. It wasn't as sunny; the colour of the popcorn changed, the music was different. Such subtle differences yet so impactful. This notion is not exclusive to just going to parks. It is a programme we are running all the time and isn't exclusive to kids. That is simply when it starts and when we learn to run our expectations program. When we expect anything and it is met, the best we can get from it is a feeling of satisfaction. When our expectations don't match our reality, we have inner conflict. We learn very quickly to judge ourselves, and if the outcome doesn't match my expectation, my experience is tainted. Therefore, there must be something wrong with me.

I remember growing up with eczema. At home, I was told, "It is OK, and it will pass." At school, I was made fun of and people wouldn't come near me. They weren't bad people they just lacked understanding. It was a condition, that's all. Yet I felt that it was my fault and something must be wrong with me on a deeper level. At home, I was told I was good looking, yet when I went to school, I was informed otherwise. We are brought up with a mismatch and the conflict starts really young.

Now external judgement plays a huge part in your inner conflict. Because when we have such mismatches we start to do things like bring in competition, and we start to compare ourselves to others who appear to have it better. When we compare ourselves to someone that has it better, we belittle ourselves. When we compare ourselves with others that appear to have "it" worse, then we can make ourselves feel better; which means we are making ourselves bigger than them. These are programmes we pick up when we are very young. It isn't like the schools do inner conflict resolution classes, is it? This is not their fault. Look how many kids have confidence issues, low self-esteem, eating disorders, it is actually frightening. After all, are we supposed to be cared for and loved at all times by our parents? Well, yes. Yet it is expressed in so many different ways that as kids we don't know what is the right way, yet we quickly learn what is the wrong way. Our experiences mismatch and create the conflicts which in turn shape our reality, our behaviour and our results, which then create further conflict. Our inner conflict.

A vicious cycle

We learn very young that inner conflict is a painful experience, albeit we don't know or call it an inner conflict. Half the time, you don't even know consciously that you are conflicted, just that something isn't right. You know that something happened and it hurts. Pain can be a great driver of change as mentioned in other chapters, yet it can be a great driver to run away, shut down and hide. Most people do the latter. Because pain hurts, it sucks. Yet displaying pain can come with greater consequences and could be displayed as a form of weakness. Physical pain is somewhat more acceptable to express, and even then we feel we have to show we are OK quickly. Emotional pain is different, not only can it be seen as weakness, most don't know how to express it. Very quickly, we judge ourselves for feeling it, we judge what people are going to say about it and, therefore, say nothing or put on a brave face. This also means we are only ever seeing one half of the truth and one half of the picture and are distorting the reality into disempowerment.

Let me ask you, when you are in pain that you can't express, are you judging yourself internally and judging what will happen externally if you express yourself? Could that mean you are running a comparison program, matching your past experience to an event in the past, reflecting on the outcome and saying nothing that could actually help you? You opt for self-punishment, I am not worthy of help so I will suffer in silence. Does that sound familiar?

Can you see why a lot of people are conflicted? Your feelings are not right or wrong, good or bad, it is simply me offering what it means to have inner conflict and what are the contributing factors to it.

To recap, when you are in pain, in judgement and punishing yourself, most people still don't open their mouths. Living like that will have continued mismatch of your reality and be very conflicted unless you address each part on a regular basis. I was working with this amazing woman called Flo. Flo was disabled, she spends most of her days in a wheelchair, and she can walk but very slowly and with the support of walking sticks. She became ill when she was very young, and for years called the disability the naughty child. She resented her disability, and she saw it as separate from her. Because she was walking around with a naughty child all the time, she could not express herself because she wanted the rest of life to be nice and easy. She felt that if she spoke up, people wouldn't take her seriously because she was disabled. She was told when she was younger to keep quiet and not upset anyone as her presence was upsetting enough. Can you imagine what that did to her? And can you understand why she called her disability the naughty child? Because it appeared to be the cause of all her problems. She carried her conflict with her for years, smiling through the pain, and more than anything, she wanted inner peace. While her disability was a major part of it, it was her environment, the people she was surrounded by and how she chose to see herself that were causing the conflict. Flo joined us for the year and worked with really owning who she was and not letting her disability define her. We did a lot of work on self-expression and renaming "The Naughty child." We worked on her self-image. I am so inspired by working with her, now not only does Flo own her disability, she also works with disabled athletes getting them fit for various competitions. She herself gets on the treadmill and does that little bit more, and last I heard she could walk over two miles unaided. Every day was a step further for her.

Do you want to know something that I find really scary? Most people don't feel that they are worthy of any help, support or guidance, that's how little they think of themselves, and that's before they even go through their judgement filter. On the other side, you have those who are in denial, stubborn and need to do everything alone, living in the scarcity mindset driven by fear. There are lots of very successful people with self-worth issues who go on to prove their worth by their achievements, and there are those who hide behind achievements in order not to deal with this. Yet all those programmes are running all the time and internally the conflict continues. You can, of course, lower your expectations in life, which will mean you won't mismatch as much, there won't be disappointment or great success: been there done that and don't want to wear the T-shirt. That is a place where the only way is down to loneliness, poverty and darkness. That's where you isolate yourself, cut off any support and take very little and safe action.

Values: the drivers of conflict

As well as everything that we have listed, our values play a huge part in our inner conflicts. Most people live to their low values and spend their time, energy and money serving their low values. That's where procrastination and frustration live, which means that you are functioning from a place of fantasy or illusion or depression. Maybe all three? Because you are not coming from a place that inspires you – your higher values. You are in a place where you need motivation because you are living your life according to other people's values, expectations, vision and purposes. Sound familiar? This ultimately means you are making yourself small because you have made other factors in your life bigger than you, such as money, job and survival. If you have made yourself smaller and are living to your low values, then you will be conflicted and the appearance of challenge will be greater than reward. The appearance of pain will be greater than pleasure, and the spiral is always downwards. Your higher values will always drive your behaviour, but you will fight against it because you don't believe that you can make money, live the life you want or be fulfilled. We are taught to be safe, educated, to get a job and live happily ever after which was someone else's model of the world and that has been inflicted onto us.

As discussed, from a very young age, we are programmed to see what is right and what is wrong. This carries through to what we perceive as our values and what is important to us.

Now if we all see the world in a different way, how can anyone have the same set of values? Most spend their lives serving other people's values while their own higher values are pushed down and denied, hence conflict within. Here your EGO kicks in. You box yourself into a perceived image and way of being, which you want to be right, which you want to serve but which creates our mismatch and conflict, resulting in an unbalanced way of living. That brings us back to seeing one-half of the truth, one-half of the picture and you not being who you truly are. In your life at present, you may feel a lot of anger, fear, resentment, jealousy, anxiety and many low vibrations, destructive and sabotaging emotions that actually have a greater effect globally.

How inner conflict impacts the world – to keep or not to keep?

Have you ever stopped to think about the greater effect living to our low values would have on the world? The word "fundamentalism" has negative connotations in the media. Fundamentalism is created by living in our low values, living in pain and with fear, resentment and jealousy. I am not saying that because you are living this way or reading this book you are a fundamentalist–I am writing this chapter so we further understand how we are doing the world and ourselves a disservice by not living to our highest values. Also because of where it can lead. There are people who are living in judgement and believe that they are right and the whole world is wrong, they feel the world owes them something. These people are largely driven by ego, fear and the need for significance. When living in such a way, you want to punish the world, and that starts inside of us.

Don't mistake a fight of justice for fundamentalism. People who are seeking justice or who are fighting injustice have an end goal that is realistic and not the destruction of anything. After all if we all lived by eye for an eye, we would all be blind. I want you to understand the extreme case of not dealing with your conflicts and how it can affect you. Fundamentalist, you may not be, but have you overreacted and found yourself thinking about extreme revenge or spiteful behaviour? The factors that create it are the same. I was working with a lady in Scotland, and her thoughts were consumed with hate and revenge. She was a good-looking lady and always had relationships. Yet the moment the guy appeared to do anything that was out of line, the guy was in for it, her reaction was of anger, victimisation, as if the world had it in for her and anyone coming into her space. She was confused too, often wanting to hurt everyone around her, anyone because she perceived everyone as having it in for her. She also perceived people not to be on her side, leading her to feel isolated. Once she calmed down, she was full of judgement because no one was there for her, which, of course, led to anger again. There was a fine line between what was going on in her head and her actually exploding.

She was behaving like a fundamentalist, the difference was she didn't go after anyone at that point. However, any longer and she was likely to do a lot of harm. We did some work on her thoughts and relaxation. Interestingly it all came from the loss of her dad and feeling like she had her perfect relationship ripped away from her. Like anything in life, it takes time and continuous effort to work through these things.

Pain is Part of the Process

Our beloved friend: pain. Something we are teaching our kids not to show. Stiff upper lip, boys don't cry. Crying is for girls. You have to protect yourself. Does any of these sound familiar? Then there are the sayings: "once bitten twice shy," "never again will I open my heart." With that comes the external notion that showing pain equals weakness.

Pain is wonderful and a powerful driver. It is a great indicator and often gives us a lot of clues before we get hit with it. Often the warning signs are there, yet most of us aren't taught how to listen and, more importantly, what to do. If anyone says that time is a healer and that's enough, I will push back very firmly. Simply because time is a healer only if you deal with the pain, that's the keyword – deal – with the pain. There are other layers involved, but it all starts with pain and embracing it as part of the process.

Pain: the driver of change

I remember the day I was standing on top of a cliff in Australia (no, I wasn't suicidal). I was staying there, in a place close to Gordon's Bay, and every day I would walk 10km from Gordon's Bay to Bondi beach and back to get some understanding and to deal with the pain I was in.

The end of my year 2009 was a good one, I had all the clients I needed to fund my trip to Australia, I had a subcontract, which ensured I had some cash flow, and I had what I thought was a beginning of a great relationship. I was flying out to see and spend some quality time working from Sydney, Australia. I was very excited and really felt like I had stepped up and made it. Little did I know that it would turn out to be one of the most painful and testing times of my life. In the grand scheme of things I had been through, it might appear minor and in the scale of world hunger it isn't a very big one. Had I been told that at the time, you would have got a different answer from me.

I have dealt with a father who is an alcoholic, being sexually molested and raped as a 12-year-old, knife fights, a Gulf war, yet none of this seemed to hurt me as much as that period. It was all part of my growth, it was all part of the universe asking me the tough questions. The question at the time I didn't want to answer yet knew I had to face. I was calling out for support yet keeping quiet. I wanted to solve everything yet give nothing away. I was feeling hurt, betrayed and alone, very alone.

That particular day was a slightly different day than my normal walks. I had some strangely uncomfortable dreams and was left with a strange feeling in my gut. I can't quite explain it: it was just a feeling that something was different, but you have no words to describe it. The world seems different, but you can't see why. It is one of those intangible times, it isn't something the left side of our brain can process. It is as if you are simply becoming an observer of yourself. With flip flops on, I started my walk, looking at the world through my painful eyes using all my coaching tools to fight it and deal with the pain and all the associated feelings that go with it. I was wondering, "How can I impact other people when I can't even deal with my own stuff? How can I leave a dent in the universe if I can't even hold myself together?" That day, I decided to stop and embrace the motion of the ocean, which was a little bit rougher than normal. I climbed over the little protective fence and stood there. I fired off my normal declarations and found myself not believing a word I was saying, I was forcing myself to say it. From then on, I went down the "why" spiral. Why isn't this working? Why me? Why does this always happen to me? Why God and universe? Why me? After all, I am a good person and good to people, why are you doing this to me? Why aren't people showing me support? Why didn't they tell me if they saw it coming? Why bother? Then the coach in me would kick in: Why am I feeling like this? Why am I not in more control?

Does this sound familiar? Have you ever used or been on the "Why" spiral? If you have, you will know that spiral is downwards, emotionally and energetically.

While I had no intention of jumping, I felt like my soul was drowning and was to be found somewhere in the pits of the ocean. Therefore, I stopped everything and stared out into the distance, sounds like a cliché; but clichés are true. I stared out into the distance and silenced the voices in my head. I simply stood there and listened, listened to waves, people walking by talking. I listened to the conversations as they ran by jogging. I could hear the seagulls screaming at each other. I found a moment of peace, really nice internal

117

peace. After a while as I sat there, one sentence came to mind and kept coming, "Elliot, pain is part of the process, accept it, don't fight it". Sitting there in peace, I listened to it again," Elliot, pain is part of the process, accept it."

To begin with, I felt myself denying it. "Not me," I started to think, and then I stopped myself and told myself to listen to the message. That's what I did, I listened. It was a very peaceful moment. I started to recall all the times I had made huge changes in my life and what was going on with me at the time. I thought about the pain I had felt when I found out my dad was an alcoholic; when my mum took the phone from him and then told me. How that day I made myself a promise never to end up like him.

Then came the blue letter day! This letter changed the course of my life for many reasons. That letter started me on a journey, which would lead me to where I am today. The impact of this letter is unquestionable, which is why I have a very powerful section that involves writing a letter in my event, *Power To Succeed*. People often underestimate the power of handwriting a letter to someone.

Blue Letter Day

The day started as a pretty normal day; I got back from school at around 3:30 and my mum told me there was a letter for me. It was a letter from my dad. I went through my normal dismissive cycle of emotions: anger, resentment, rejection and hate.

"I have no interest in what he has to say, none whatsoever," I told my mum (in reality I was telling myself). Except this time on the envelope it stated: *please read*. He had never done that before. Maybe he actually died, I thought. Maybe he was sending me money for the first time in years. I opened it and started to read, it had the normal apologies from a dad to a son and a request for me to give him another chance with a ticket to England to see him. He wasn't dead nor was it money. It was a flight to England; I hadn't been there since I was 12, on my way to Argentina. I was then a pain in the backside. Because of my behaviour when I was 12, I also felt it would be a good time to show everyone how much I had changed, as I was now 16. At the time, more than anything I just saw it as a holiday and a chance to shop. Little did I see or know the significance of this journey to England that would completely change my direction and where I was heading in life.

The day you make a life-changing decision.

There was nothing really special about my flight over to England, and I can't say I remember much of being picked up. I do remember getting to my dad's living arrangements. One room, which he was sharing with my brother, in a place shared with a transvestite in the room next to us and a Scottish mum and her son across the hall. The first night my dad sat down with me and said, "Elli I am an alcoholic, I have been since I was 13. I want you to see me for who I really am, no masks, no drink – just me your dad. I have been clean now for a few months and will be going in for treatment. What you do with this is up to you," and he shook my hand.

I went to sleep. I am not sure if I was dreaming or deep in thought when this came up. I kept thinking over and over again, "One day I will have to bury him, don't you want to know who you will be burying?" What a strange thought, I remember thinking, yet it kept on circling around in my head.

For the next few days, I spent my time connecting with family and seeing old friends of the family. One friend called Nick introduced me to heavy metal, which I fell in love with. He also introduced me to some of his friends and some very lovely Essex girls. I started to see how I could have a life here, people were pretty cool, and I had a passport that would make coming back easy. Once again that thought kept coming back: "Don't you want to know your dad when the day comes and you have to bury him?" The more I hung around in London, the more I knew coming back to live in England was the right thing to do, and yes, I did want to know who my dad was, really know who he was. It was done. I declared my intention to come back and live in the UK.

Let me tell you this was no easy decision. Socially, I had everything, what a change from when I was 12 to 15. I had a group of friends who I was very close to and would hang out with. For my 16th birthday, I had two surprise birthday parties. I was sought after by a fair few women, I had my own phone line in my room. Socially, things were very good. Besides that factor, I didn't have a lot going for me.

In school, I was pretty much heading to be a failure, which meant the job I might be able to get would be labour or very minimal. I wasn't going to be much in the army because of all my health conditions. If I could make a living based on being popular, then I would have thought much harder. At the age of 16, I made the decision, *I am going back to live in London! I am going to go and get to know my dad, save my education and all will be good.*

With much sadness in my heart and with a lot of love, I left Israel. I was given a pile of goodbye letters, which I still have, and lots of love. I landed in England, a sad and hopeful man. This was my new beginning. A new start for me, for my relationship with my dad and maybe even my brother and, of course, education.

I still find it funny that the first thing we did when I got picked up was buy a kebab, it still makes me smile. We drove back to the one-bedroom place where we would all share the space for a month. Even though I was staying in North London, I spent pretty much my first month travelling up to Essex to hang out with the people I had met on my previous visit. Then life kicked in. I was to register for school, I couldn't get into the Jewish Free School because they wanted rabbinical proof that my parents were divorced, my response to that was short and swift. *Fuck off.* We registered at a normal local school, which is where my re-education started. My dad went into treatment, and my brother and I moved in together.

I learnt very quickly about the division in groups, rockers

hang with rockers. At the time, it was ravers, ravers hang with ravers and very rarely do they mix. Considering I was one of the only rockers in the school, Jewish and from Israel, my little isolated-self came back, I became withdrawn and quiet. It didn't help living with my brother, who kept making out that he didn't have any money to give me. Somehow, he always found money for beer. When I pointed it out to him he took a swing at me, so I ducked, punched him in the face and threw him on the couch. Until this day, I don't think he has forgiven me for that. I walked out for the night and went to stay with a family friend. That was the beginning of my brother and I living together. Great start!

It is safe to say that people weren't really queuing up to speak to me. Also, because of my failure in school, I had to take my GCSEs for the first time. The class I was in wasn't your normal class. It was for "special people" which basically meant it was for people who didn't pass their GSCEs and needed to re-sit or had ADD. Some of the guys in there were fairly rough, and I did my best to befriend them; it was a slow process, but eventually they started inviting me places and I thought I was in until I threw a house party. When they all showed up, they drunk lots, stole every CD in the house, even my housemate's pager! Welcome to England Elliot, and welcome to not fitting in.

I later found out that was the plan all along and that they never really wanted to be my friends. We live and learn. After the party, we made some threats about going to the police, and we had most of our things returned, and I got punched for the effort too. It was safe to say that going back to Israel seemed like a very good move, and I remember picking up the phone to my mum and crying my heart out and making tapes (they were around) for my friends whom I missed dearly. One of them would come to see me that year so I would have something to look forward to. After I had that chat with my mother, for the first time my brother sat me down and opened up to me. He offered me his encouragement and told me to stick it out.

That week, I saw an advert for auditions for a play: *As You Like it* by Shakespeare. Everyone thought I was weird anyway. What better way to find other weirdoes to hang out with than in a play?

Something else I started doing was cross-country running, once again I was told that I had a natural talent for it and it gave me access to some pretty cool guys too. I got a small part in the play, but I got more than that. I got the key to a whole new social group, people, who accepted me and my quirky self. From that, I was asked to audition for the school production of *Grease*. Once again, a monumental event as it set further on the path that led me to where I am today.

I stayed with my brother for six months until my mother came over. Being consistent, school studies weren't going great, no one could really read my handwriting, and I felt I was misunderstood a lot. I also managed to have a fistfight with one of the teachers who decided to corner me and threaten me, so I did what every 17-year-old would do; I punched him, he punched back, I punched harder and faster. My street side was woken up.

Sadly the school didn't see it that way, I was sent home and called back the next day to explain. I went back the next day and explained what had happened but wasn't believed. They sent me home again until I got "my story straight." That took a week. My saving grace was that by the time I had the fight with the teacher, I had represented the school in local and national championships. Winning various places in the group competitions, not so much in the individual side, I had done *As You Like It,* a Fashion show (me a model ...) and was about to do *Grease*. They told me that as I had been such a good ambassador for the school, there would be no further action if I wrote the teacher an apology letter. The alternative was to be expelled. Guess what I did? I wrote the letter.

Writing the letter meant I could do *Grease*. By the time I performed in *Grease*, I pretty much had made my mind up that I was going after Performing Arts. My GCSEs were a lost cause; I got 2 Es, one F and one U if you are unfamiliar with this marking. A B and C are the pass marks, E and F are different degrees of failure, and U is so bad they can't even give it a mark. What I did do was get into a College for Performing Arts unconditionally.

The next two years were interesting. I formed some amazing friendships and had some challenging times, and then I thought that a career in musical theatre was the way forward. The challenge was that my singing voice wasn't the greatest, my dancing was OK and my acting was average. I took singing lessons to improve, gave up dairy and worked hard on acting. The best thing that happened from giving up dairy was that I didn't get hay fever anymore and the eczema on my arms cleared up. What a great side benefit!

At the end of the two years, I auditioned for a couple of musical schools and didn't get in. The only other choice at the time was university to do Dance and Drama.

I continued to think when I was struggling with my studies at university, struggling to connect with people and let people in, that if I didn't deal with the pain of the rape, a part of me would remain closed off. I remembered the day when I was stuck in Barcelona with no cash and none of my debit/credit cards working to get the train home. I remembered committing to create a better future for myself. The list was long, yet there was one common thread. Pain was part of the process! Pain was part of the process when I was learning to become a dancer, why would it be any different now? Just because I was a little wiser, I would be exempt from the very laws that govern our growth? The very laws that govern the universe. Did I really think that I was part of some special club that skipped people like me because I was a good person? What I noticed at that moment was, of course, this was part of the process; more than that I noticed that I was asking a whole different set of questions and they weren't judgemental. The questions I was asking myself were more solution based and moving forward. I had felt something shift inside me. There were lightness and relief. The journey was not done yet, there was still a long way to go. I couldn't define what had happened. I felt like I had taken a huge emotional dump, although, like any wounded person, the journey of healing was still a way to go. Something inside me had sparked, and it felt different and refreshing from all the down spiralling energy I was swinging in. It felt like I had learnt to swim again or to take a deep breath, and it felt good.

Knowing that I had to face everyone back in our house, I started my walk home. I didn't know that four hours had passed by, and I had caught a tan. I had got my soul back from the ocean, cleansed and refreshed. I knew that I was heading for some big changes and some tough times. I had no idea what they were but felt a little bit more ready by simply understanding that pain and accepting it are part of the process.

Fighting pain is tiring and emotionally consuming. It was that emotional pain that led me to the cliff, accepting that pain as part of the process allowed me to let go of it and create space to heal.

Pain – the driver of change

Now think of the darkest moment you have ever had. Think about the most painful experiences you have ever had: did it prompt you to change? And make big changes? My experience in Australia prompted me to make some big, big changes, it prompted me to reassess my whole life, and I still maintain that I am one of the lucky ones. Even though it took around one and half years to turn my life around.

At the core of change was pain. Had I not turned it round, I would have not succeeded. I would have suffered the pain of being another coach that didn't make it. The pain that I wouldn't impact the world and help to make it a better place. The pain that I would be like my dad. Either way, the pain of staying the same was greater than the pain of changing. More than anything I knew that if I gave up, I would make it about me and short change myself of the chance to make a difference.

As I have mentioned, I have dealt with a lot in my time on this earth. The biggest pain changer for me was my time in Australia. Turning it around there was still plenty of pain, nothing would match that month I had. In that month, within a couple of weeks I went from coaching five clients to one, now keep in mind that all those clients had paid up front for their coaching, and I was depending on them carrying on with me as cash flow. I had used their payments for Australia, now is the time you are allowed to think, silly boy. I was using their money to fund my business trip to Australia, and it was a business trip. I had a sub contract with another company, which would have provided cash flow that I needed to keep going and give me some spare cash.

Just before I found myself standing on the edge of the cliff there was another spanner in the works. The day started out like most days, I jumped on the phone to start my role with the subcontracting company, only to be stopped with a request to speak over Skype, which I did immediately. What happened next, I didn't see coming. By this point while working for these guys subcontracting, I had made them over £30k in less than a month in ticket sales and sponsorship deals. Even though I was on the other side of the world, I had worked out a timetable, and all the times zones that would mean that the people in the UK wouldn't notice where I was. It was all good, except it wasn't. My subcontracting company had paid me for November, nothing for December and reassured me that I would be paid, as they were friends, I believed them. I went off to Australia and still no money. There were a few exchanges of emails and then came the killer blow and email simply stating, "Let's talk over Skype." My gut was telling me this was not good news, and if I have learnt something it is to listen to your gut. It was further re-enforced when the week before we had arranged to have our normal Skype chat, they didn't turn up for it with no email or message to apologise. The writing was on the wall and in big bold letters.

That wasn't the only writing which was on the wall. A big part of my going to Australia was because of a girl, a girl who I had liked for months and was finally making progress. When the opportunity came along to travel out to Australia for both business and pleasure (or love in this case), I was in. When I arrived in Australia, everything was amazing for one day and this was New Year's Eve. I travelled for two days across the world for meetings and to see her. In my mind, it was the beginning of something amazing and new. It was certainly a new beginning for us both: for me to face the pain that was coming to create the change that needed to happen and for her to start her new job with a billionaire. The job was always on the cards, and from my second day, I knew my time with her was numbered. He told her to choose, the job or me. She chose the job. Suddenly there was no room for me in her life. All her focus was on this new job, which was what she told me, and I believed it. However, it was a slow and painful process. New Year's Eve was lovely, and then at the stroke of midnight, I put my arm around her and she stepped away from the grip of my arm. Sign number one.

Although nothing had been said, she started withdrawing and pulling away emotionally and became cold. Sign number two. Then every time the phone rang and it was him she would light up. Sign number three. Oh, yeah, $20,000 earrings to welcome her to the team. Sign number four.

I must say that at no point did she make any promises about me travelling out there. It was a case of let's go out there and see. Then came the walk, the talk and the end of our short relationship. That was within the first 10 days. Ouch. Well, at least I had my coaching clients, right? Well, one by one, they all stated how well they were doing and were ready to fly and have a go on their own. One by one they left me. No girl, down to one client, and at least, I had my subcontracting client, right? Then came the Skype call. "Well, Elliot, things really aren't working out, we should have gone with someone with more sales experience." *What the f**k are you on about?* I thought. We didn't agree on targets, we agreed on time and hours, and I knew I had produced results. They weren't interested and hung up.

Two weeks in, no girl, one coaching client and no payment from subcontracting, which amounted to £3,000, the amount I needed to get by and cover costs.

All that translated to no money, a broken heart and stuck on the other side of the world in a lot of pain, a lot of emotional pain. It was out and out horrible. Days after I landed back in the UK, it was my birthday, and I hated it. It was a horrible birthday, I felt like I had lost everything. No money, and I meant no money, no girl, no clients. It was serious question time. How much did I want it? Things had to change. I refused to blame anyone but me. Here is what a lot of people tend to do – they switch to blame mode. I could have blamed her and come up with lots of stories, blamed her for making me go across the world to be with her and then dumping me for a billionaire. I could have blamed my clients for being ungrateful for all the extra miles I went for them and not sticking with me. As for the company who didn't pay me, well there were certainly things I could have done differently. I did go after them legally but didn't invest a lot of effort into them. Therefore, I decided I could deal with me, I could not change anything or anyone. I could control how I chose to show up. That month started me off with the biggest change and self-assessment I have ever had to undertake, the pain of that month made me look at everything I stood for, lived for and wanted in life. I had to look at all my beliefs and programming; I had to look at my belief system and my confidence; I had to look at my whole approach to business and being an entrepreneur, and I had to look at my relationship with money and with love.

I am well aware that I didn't lose a limb. However, to watch my whole world collapse on me hurt a lot! The pain I experienced in that month actually made me a better coach, speaker, businessmen and even boyfriend. It didn't happen overnight and took months of me going in deep, very, very, very deep and it still continues. Because I understood that at the time my driver for change was the pain I was experiencing and actually it was driving and accelerating my results. This happened because I dealt with my pain, I dealt with it through various coaches and support. I kept talking about it and focused all my efforts on turning this around to become a success. I went into creative overflow and was churning out product after product, I started to study various marketing techniques and to talk more about my purpose in life and tell more people about my story and who I was vs. a coach who is doing a talk.

The first six months of the year were horrible, yet it was the pain that was driving my growth and change. It was actually elevating me to the next level as a coach and as a businessman. I was not willing to give up and give in. This was not an option, the only option was success! I found a couple of corporate contracts that gave me some income, and at least I could pay my rent and live for a few months. Also, a couple of friends loaned me some money to tide me over. All my energy and focus went into rebuilding myself, my business and my coaching. Had this not happened, I would have accepted a much smaller role in this place, this universe. I came up with a system to do it, which included a mixture of coaching tools and my take on it. When addressing it and looking deep, I would break it down into this:

Perception – what am I choosing to see?

Memory – what have I attached to the event?

Imagination – what was I creating vs. what was happening, what were the feelings, actions and results because of it?

Intuition – find the feelings around the pain, what is my gut saying about it?

Reason – what meaning am I choosing to attach to it?

Will – where is my focus, and how much do I want it?

It looked like this:

Perception – what am I choosing to see? I am choosing to see that I am isolated, that everyone has it in for me and that I am going to fail again. I am choosing not to see the point of anything and am feeling sorry for myself. Instead, I want to see the people who are there for me, the people who are lending me the money to live and the people who turned out to celebrate my birthday. There were over 30 people there.

Memory – What have I attached to the event? I have brought all my memories into this one, the memories of being hurt by other women, and it is happening again, I am choosing to attach the memory of pain to the last few months. I am attaching the memory of failure to the situation.

Imagination – what was I creating vs. what was happening, what were the feelings, actions, and results because of it? I was creating the illusion that no one cared, that everything that happened was planned and everyone was in on it. What was happening was people didn't really know, people might have suspected, but they didn't know. People do care, but they are torn because they know both of us. My clients, good on them, it was time for them to fly. I am creating a feeling of resentment and missing out on the feeling of love and support around me. I have gone into hiding and have disappeared, wanting to believe that no one cares. On the other hand, look at how creative I have been.

Intuition – find the feelings around the pain, what is my gut saying about it? My gut is saying this will pass, it's hurt now, it's part of the process and beyond this lays your greatest achievement.

Reason – what meaning am I choosing to attach to it? The meaning I am choosing to give this is that it is unfair, and I am destined to be like my dad. Which already is not true based on results

Will – where is my focus and how much do I want it? My focus is on turning this situation around and becoming an even greater coach, boyfriend and making more money than ever before. Even if a part of me wants to prove everyone wrong.

These were my answers to the questions at the time. I suggest that you stop reading now, choose a situation and fill in your own answers ...

Pain doesn't equal suffering

A simple notion, but a very interesting one here in the West. You see while I am talking about pain, it is part of the process and driver of change. The fact is, you don't need to suffer while you are in pain. In the West, it has become a bit of a custom to associate pain to suffering, why is that? And it seems to be often chosen by the masses. A lot of people take on the notion that the more you display suffering, the more attention you will get and the more you can get away with. We have learnt through years of conditioning that when you are in pain you have to suffer for a long period of time. We also carry that forward with our emotional pain. Still think it is a strange notion? Think of all the drama queens you know. Think of the people you know that are living in excuses, I bet you they are suffering from some sort of condition. Now I will say this again, this isn't to say when we are in pain we don't suffer, we do. I am talking about people whose suffering seems to last a lifetime.

When I was working as a corporate trainer, I was put in charge of running goal setting workshops with gold-winning Olympians, both able-bodied and Para Olympians. This was just after London won the bid for the Olympics, One of the sessions was led by Vicky Hansford. She was an incredibly inspiring woman. Vicky was diagnosed with cancer and lost part of her right leg. She had also lost part of her lungs as well. As part of her recovery, she started rowing. Vicki started rowing in February 2006. And she went on to win medals – at the time, she had won one in Beijing. Her story was very inspiring, and it was a great session for all involved. While doing the workshop, she discussed something called Phantom Limb Syndrome:

A **phantom limb** is a sensation that an amputated or missing limb (even an organ, like the appendix) is still attached to the body and is moving appropriately with other body parts.

Approximately 60 to 80% of individuals with an amputation experience phantom sensations in their amputated limb, and the majority of the sensations are painful.

Phantom sensations may also occur after the removal of body parts other than the limbs, e.g. after amputation of the breast, extraction of a tooth (phantom tooth pain) or removal of an eye (phantom eye syndrome). The missing limb often feels shorter and may feel as if it is in a distorted and painful position. Occasionally, the pain can be made worse by stress, anxiety, and weather changes. Phantom limb pain is usually intermittent. The frequency and intensity of attacks typically decline with time.

Although not all phantom limbs are painful, patients will sometimes feel as if they are gesturing, feel itches, twitch, or even try to pick things up. For example, Ramachandran and Blakeslee describe that some people's representations of their limbs do not actually match what they should be, for example, one patient reported that her phantom arm was about "six inches too short".

A slightly different sensation known as phantom pain can also occur in people who are born without limbs, and people who are paralyzed. Phantom pains occur when nerves that would normally innervate the missing limb cause pain. It is often described as a burning or similarly strange sensation and can be extremely agonizing for some people, but the exact sensation differs widely for individuals. Other induced sensations include warmth, cold, itching, squeezing, tightness, and tingling.[3]

When someone loses an arm, they still reach out to scratch it as if it was there and a lot of times they feel the same pain. Why is that? Is it for the simple reason that a person has an attachment to their arm? It is a pretty safe statement to make. One might also say that they have a pretty good reason to suffer, yet you watch anyone who has gone through a huge physical trauma, the last thing they want to do is suffer any more. How does this relate? Simple: most

---

[3] http://en.wikipedia.org/wiki/Phantom_limb

people walk around suffering as if both their arms, legs and feet have been cut off. They choose to suffer; it always amazes me, why would you choose that? Would the choice be to get over it and get on with your life? You would think so. What happens is that when we are in emotional pain, we attach a lot of judgement to the event. Think of the last time you were in serious pain. When it was physical pain, stop and think about the thought process you went through. You had physical pain going on, and the next step was not to show it, right? Or when you did display it, you showed everyone how much you were in pain and how much you were suffering. Now that is OK, when you are in pain show it by all means, no point putting on a brave face, it is when you play on it and use it to manipulate that I may have a bone to pick with you.

None of this is written in judgement of you. I am writing this because part of the reason people stay in pain for longer than needed is because they choose to suffer. People carry on suffering for years and become martyrs. This happens because when we show pain we get sympathy or people show us some love and support. We like that. The next time that happens, we might play on it a little bit more. Then we play on it again until it becomes a pattern of behaviour. Now this isn't something that happens on a conscious level. This happens much, much deeper than that. Like any behaviour, this is learned. It is a conditioned response. Here is a surprise for you, we learnt that when we were babies. When you wanted something, you cried, then when you didn't get something you cried again and, of course when you were in pain you cried. When we were little kids, we tested it some more on those big people we called adults. Then we learnt how to get away with it some more. There were lots of times when we were generally in pain, but we let the suffering carry on for a bit longer. That's how we learnt to associate pain with suffering. This isn't to say that when you are in pain it doesn't hurt. I am talking about the victim or martyrdom that goes with it.

When you accept the situation and stop seeing yourself as a victim, you are sending your mind a whole different set of messages. You are sending instructions, which create the space for healing, deep emotional healing. If you are stuck in the cycle of suffering, you are sending your consciousness the messages that you are still in pain, and thus delay the healing process. Our mind is like the biggest kid driving the biggest engine of our body, this kid knows no right or wrong. This kid only knows exactly what you tell it and messages you are giving it. If you are sending the message you are in pain emotionally and suffering, the kid will give you more to suffer about. If you send it different messages, messages of intent to deal and recover, it will point you in that direction.

By choosing to suffer, you are in effect carrying around and wearing extra layers of heavy, smelly, itchy clothes. Suffering is a choice. People always have an issue with this concept when I mention it at my seminars. Because, believe it or not, people are happy to suffer and to stay stuck because it is easier than actually dealing with the issues at hand. Think about it, how many times have you used an injury as an excuse? Or delayed doing something? Even worse, didn't take action to address an issue because you had / have a "condition." Like a bad back, I have one too, it has never stopped me from doing anything. Bad knees, yep, had one of them too and still had a dance career. Asthma, yep, got that too, still run twice a week, bad hips, bad shoulders, etc. ... This isn't about denial of the challenges these conditions can pose. It is about finding a way to work with them and have a successful, active life. Just like Flo.

I have worked with ex-offenders, and they loved suffering and living with the suffer button on. Some of them would rather suffer, keep a health condition going so they could keep their benefits going and not have to get a job. The best example for this case was Flo. Flo learnt to accept her condition, which was a spinal cord injury, which she used to reject and refer to as the bad child that stopped her from doing and achieving. Flo learnt to work with her condition and to stop suffering from it. Once she started to do that, she actually found a job as a personal trainer, something Flo always wanted to do and is living the life she wants.

As for the offenders, the place was outside London, in Slough. I remember walking into the room. They were sat around the table with their "show me what you got attitude," and after telling them a little bit of my story we started to connect. We had an open discussion about their situations, and there were a variety of offenders in the room, mainly violent ones. When they told me about their situation, I challenged them, "Why are you choosing to suffer?" "It's not a choice it's a reality," they would reply.

"How are you choosing to suffer?" I would question back. "How are you making the situation worse than it already is?" Stunned silence. At this point, I got them to write down their answers. You could see things starting to change slowly, "But Elliot, people don't give second chances." "All people? Are there people who have criminal pasts and are now successful, yes or no?" "Yes," they replied. "How long will you carry on being martyrs for?" I asked. Even more shifts started to happen, it was a challenging day met with reward. At the end of the day, each and every one of them came up to me and thanked me for my time, energy and for shaking them up. The following week, I got this email, I have removed the name as the person requested to remain anonymous:

Elliot did a great job of explaining cause and effect, and it's by taking action that you can be a cause rather than being the victim (effect) of your circumstances or your past.

'Mind your own business' means taking action on things that are within your control and letting go of thinking about matters and circumstances beyond your control; if you clutter up your mind with blame, shame, fault or judgemental thoughts then thinking gets clouded; no action gets taken, and we get stuck in a negative thought spiral which leads to stress and depression. If you are not part of the solution, you are part of the problem so please keep taking action and don't be afraid to get things wrong. See failure as feedback, as with feedback you can take different action as a result of the new knowledge. I will stop using the saying 'the only failure is never to try' and replace it

with the only failure is never to take action, as try is a weak word, and as we saw with Violet trying to pick up the chair, we either do or we don't; and trying only gives you a sore back!

The next email was an update:

Person one has done great (best of them all) he is at 2nd interview stage and talks about a distinction called 'mind your language' which was his key takeaway from workshop – Person two has a plan although he is still in the drama of his reduced benefit due to a combined benefit claim with girlfriend – Person three is writing his own job spec to volunteer. Person four admitted he is lazy and is thinking about what actions he can take to overcome this.

Thanks again for your loving support

I have done the same work with people who haven't offended and still decide to suffer in order to get away with doing less or not going to work. Once we work together, I shift them out of this mindset or walk away from them. Is this how someone who wants a great life, high standards and wants to change would behave? No! Therefore, I won't work with people who choose to suffer as a long-term solution. I only work with people who choose to deal with the suffering and pain they have been through, to free them up to have the life they truly want. Now that's better.

University – The emergence of an Icon

This would be a good time to roll back the years a bit and talk about university. At university, I maintained my rocker status throughout and had really long hair.

One of the biggest moments at university came when I watched Rudolf Nureyev dance. That day everything changed for me. The moment I saw him dance, I felt all my physiology light up, my heart beat faster and I was mesmerised. He was everything I wanted to be as a dancer. He had an amazing story: he was told he would never make it, and he did. He changed the face of dancing and the role of the male dancer. He had passion, an amazing jump and was globally famous.

Nureyev's influence was immediate. I started to live and breathe dance. While most people would come home pissed and watch the football, I came home drunk and watched him dance. I read everything there was to read about him, and he became my inspiration to become a dancer.

I started spending hours in the studio, just me and a tape player, dancing, choreographing and attempting to master the craft. I attended as many dance classes as I could. There was, however, one problem: I had never been taught how to dance, and the teachers at that university had no interest in teaching it. I knew I had to up my game if I was to become a dancer like Nureyev.

Keep in mind that at this point I was 21, my body was pretty set and, of course, I had no real dance technique or experience. I gained a little from the two years I was at university, but nowhere near enough, and there was still one big problem in the quest of becoming a dancer: I had no technique. I made a bold declaration to everyone: "I am going to leave university at the end of my second year and go to dance school."

Most people laughed, some people told me to finish university first, including my mum. The teachers made a point of telling me that I wouldn't get in. They told me I was too old. They also told me that even if I did get in, I wouldn't get noticed. They told me my body was wrong for a dancer. They even said my long hair would put them off. I didn't want to know, and I wanted out of university.

Having had a fight a few months into the year didn't help my desire to stay at university. More than that, I knew that if I wanted to become a dancer, I had to go where dancers went and where real dance teachers were teaching and where I could learn dance technique. I was up against it because I would be competing against younger and far more experienced dancers. Also, I would get no funding and would have to work every night and weekend to make ends meet. I would have to work harder than every student there because I was older and had no real experience.

Would all that stand in the way of my dream? Did Nureyev let people stop him? The answer was a definite NO! In my heart and soul, I was going to give this my best shot, and if it didn't work out, I had my third year at university to fall back on.

Here's the thing, nothing felt more depressing than going

back to university for the third year. I treated it like there was no way back, and truly there wasn't! I had some good friends at university but beside that I didn't have much, sound familiar? Where did that show up in my life previously? At the last time I left somewhere to pursue a different future.

Taking a Risk is the Beginning

I remember the day I set foot in my dance school, which was located in Leeds in Yorkshire, I also remember the uncertainty that surrounded it. At this point, I had no money, no idea how I would fund the first couple of years if I got in or even If I would. Do you know that notion of not knowing how? Just that you have to do it. I had worked on a solo to perform but I didn't actually choreograph anything because every time I attempted to do some choreographing, the music would carry me away. Sounds corny, right? Well, It is true.

At the dance school I made an executive decision, I decided I would let the music take over at the audition and express myself that way. I just hoped that I would get asked to repeat it.

I arrived at the school nice and early and was greeted by these big grey doors. I stopped outside, took a deep breath and walked in. The moment I stepped into the school, everything felt right and light. I proceeded into the main theatre where we were greeted and given our name tag, yep, just like in *Fame* (remember the TV Program?) or *X-Factor*. The school principal made an announcement that threw me a little, "Welcome to your audition for the 3rd year of dance training!" *What the fuck?* I thought. Third year? I wasn't auditioning for the third year. Apparently, I was now. She carried on, "We would like to welcome the whole class of dance students from Newcastle, how nice to see you all again." What the hell? Here I am auditioning at a level I am nowhere near with a class of students that have spent two years together. You see sometimes things just don't show up the way we thought they would or expected. Has this happened to you?

Well, it turns out there were three more students beside myself who weren't part of the class. Everyone else was well-toned, and they all looked like dancers. I looked like I was straight out of a rock concert, long hair, big glasses and no shape to my body. Away we went. We went straight into the ballet audition, which is safe to say was a complete mess! I didn't know any of the terms of what they meant and was always a step behind everyone else at the bar. The ballet teacher kept stopping and looking at me through his glasses, saying nothing just glaring at me. I felt very small. I also kept saying to myself, whatever happens just keep kicking higher than anyone else. The only thing I had left was my jump. *Whatever happens*, I said, *when it comes to jump, just jump higher than everyone else, just keep jumping, forget your feet, just keep jumping*! That's what I did. It was clear I was out of my depth here.

Then came the next section. I remember in the break thinking, *throw yourself into everything. Take risks and be big and keep going whatever happens.* That's how I approached the next section. At this point, the teacher noticed my struggle and my fight. He would stop and check if I were following. I was getting noticed. I kept up with the attitude. I was undoubtedly out of place and out of my depth. It was obvious that I didn't belong in the third year.

The question was did I belong there at all? Sometimes doubt can start to creep in and it ends up being a distraction and can take us out or knock us off course.

Then came the solo section. I sat and watched all these really brilliant dancers one by one go up and do their stuff. Then they called my number, and the music started. I can only remember little bits of it. The music simply flew through me, and I let it take over me. I surrendered to it. It felt peaceful, yet I was moving. I felt moved yet calm. From the inside, it was a beautiful experience. I was dancing like I didn't have a care in the world, like the saying. Dance like no one is watching. Then came the moment when the music faded out. That was it. Audition over.

At that point, there was an announcement: "Thank you, everyone, for coming, we will go out and have a discussion about you all. We will return with who is going to get an offer. Please keep in mind that we only have four places left so the competition is tight."

From that moment onwards it was like a scene from a movie. There was a deadly silence in the room. You could hear the seconds tick away. Tick tock tick tock, it felt like a scene from a horror movie when the arms of the clock dictate what happens next. At any given moment, Jason from *Friday the 13th* will jump out. It was that tense. Time passed very slowly. To my eyes, time had slowed right down and the seconds hand on the clock simply got heavier and heavier. My heartbeat could be heard all the way back in London, faster and louder than ever. Suddenly a girl burst out crying. Even through the sobbing and the tears, the silence felt louder and time simply wasn't going any quicker.

I should add that the theatre was in a converted synagogue. Because it was a registered building, they had kept all the art from the synagogue and the windows were full of symbols and images from the Old Testament. I found myself looking at the Star of David and asking the higher power to help me now and I would forever have faith. I kept repeating it like an affirmation. The doors opened, and the judges stood at the back of the theatre.

The speaker was brief and to the point: "As we said, we only have four places this year. So the people who are going through are ..." she reeled off four numbers and none of them was mine.

I was gutted and dropped my head into my arms, my old beliefs kicked in: "I never get the big breaks," said my voice in my head. I found myself giving myself a forehead slap. As my hand touched my forehead, I heard, "and we want to speak to number ..." and they called my number. I jumped out of my seat and ran to the back of the theatre to talk to them. "Well, you aren't good enough to go into the third year, we would like to invite you to come into the first year, does that interest you?" My answer was YES. "You will have no funding from us or the government, how will you pay the fees?" My answer was, "I will do whatever it takes! What ever it takes! I will work every night and weekend if I have to! I promise." There it is again, I didn't know how, I just knew I would! We will write to you and make you an offer and, by the way, you have a lot to prove," Yes, I did, to myself, to my family, to everyone that told me not to go for it and to everyone that had supported me. I was over the moon! My real dance career had begun and now I could follow in the footsteps of my hero and idol. I was 21, broke with no savings, my family had no money. I was about to drop out of university to start again, and I had no idea how I would make it happen, it didn't matter. Sometimes, we don't know the how, it is that moment you must put everything you have into making it work.

The first couple of months were tough; I danced all day and then went to work in a local pub, which simply ended up burning me out. One day, I had a meltdown in class, I had no balance at all. I stormed out of the class in tears and went to the office of a lovely lady to have a chat. I say have a chat, I was balling my eyes out, unsure how I could carry on with no sleep, no energy and no money. She listened and simply said, "Elliot keep going, you are making an impression here, and you are never late and work very hard. This isn't going unnoticed!"

Later that day, I found out they were considering me for a Fee Wave, which, in effect was a scholarship. I had hope and faith again. I went back to class and carried on working hard for a couple of weeks. Then the big day came, and I was informed that I got it. It was the first day that I have ever felt real reward for my hard work and that people really had faith in me, I felt like a million bucks. I graduated with a job with a small dance company, 99% attendance, zero lateness and a degree. Something none of my family, let alone me, thought I would ever have.

At times in your journey, there will be what appear to be dead ends and a path that leads nowhere. Keep this in mind, you never know who is watching you and what you mean to other people. At some point, you simply let go and have complete trust that it will work out.

I had a dancing career for five years, which was a mixture of pain, being broke and touring various parts of the world. During that time, I used teaching as a method of income and looking back this was where my coaching really started. I was also homeless for nine months living on my dad's living room floor while I got work. It started off being a month, then I got a job for seven months in Germany and then a different job ended and I came back to the UK.

I was so in debt and couldn't afford to pay the rent. So much for the glamour of being a dancer. It didn't matter to me where I was sleeping as long as I was dancing and getting to class to train. It didn't matter what job I did in between jobs as long as I was dancing. My dancing career came to an end one Monday morning after a year out with a back injury. During that year, I did more choreography and freelance teaching than actually dancing.

This Monday was going to be my comeback day. I had stopped drinking anything that was bad for me, I stretched every day and worked out. Picture a montage from Rocky getting fit, except mine lasted three months. The Monday had arrived and I was very excited. I got to class and did my stretches. I was strong and in good shape, I thought. We got through the whole class and then came the last exercise. A kick and jump. As I kicked my leg up, my back went from beneath me.

It literally feels like someone has put their fist in your back and is twisting a dial that is locking your back in place. I dropped straight to my knees and cried in pain. I had to crawl to the back of the room. The teacher came over and asked if I was OK. No, I wasn't, not because of pain that was painful, it was more the realisation that actually this was the beginning of the end and that dance wasn't going to be part of my life for much longer. If only I had the tools then that I do now I would still be dancing. Hindsight is a great thing. I was now thirty, renting a room from a friend and still broke, with no career and everything I worked so hard for was gone. Everything that I fought for was now in the past. Along the path you get to certain milestones, you will get to a certain level and achieve some of your goals, yet life has a funny way of keeping us grounded and kicking us into shape. Normally that comes without a warning. As that happens, it might feel like there is no hope, no reason to keep going. Everything I wanted to do crashed. I went to a very dark place in my mind and then simply went into autopilot. Ever been through the days simply going through the motions with no direction and having lots of questions swirling around in your head? Why me? What now? Everything I was is no longer! What do I do now? The truth was I lost some of my identity that day too. I had a go at different treatments and made some progress, I did a lot of strengthening as well. Then I had an x-ray, which showed a disc hernia; I had ground down my discs through my years as a dancer. I had really flexible hips and tight back and as a result I would over-compensate using my hips where I would be using my back and that ground down the discs in my lower back. I remember him saying, "It will never be good, but we can get it to work. If one was the best and four was the worst, you are at a three in terms of damage. The first thing you need to do is STOP everything." Keep in mind that up until that day I had been working out, dancing and working with my body every day. That's like telling a professional footballer not to play, a professional runner not to run or a musician not to play his favourite instrument. While everything appeared lost, it was simply paving the way for something else in my life. Just reading this book now might be paving a new path for you in your life.

I did stop for three months and then had some failed attempts at getting back into dance. Here is the irony, when I got injured, never before had I got so many calls about jobs. They were coming from everywhere. Most dancers dream of the day they won't have to audition for roles, I had got there except I couldn't cash in on it or take them up because of my back. At the time, I didn't have the resources or tools that I have now, the only thing I could do was walk away from the one thing that gave me direction.

My mind went into overdrive.

From then on it was a roller coaster of business ventures, different jobs and professions. I hadn't lost my hard work attitude, strong mind and my ability to use my energy to be creative, which saw me start a fashion label that never really took off, put on and compare fashion shows, turn to TV presenting that didn't go beyond a TV show reel. I wrote a TV show, which actually got some attention from a production company and even got checked out by a big TV station only to be told the timelines wouldn't work. I did PR for a modelling agency for a year and doubled its database and its status, ran bars in theatres, worked in bars and managed cafés. I went back to the TV show a year later and put money into making a demo, which was a disaster. I put on a property exhibition show that actually was a success and might have been the way forward, and in some way it has been as I still put on events such as *Power To Succeed!* You may not always understand where a path is leading at the time.

What did happen was that I found my way into training, which I still do, and from training I found my way into coaching, entrepreneurship and building the business that I am running today. It is true that sometimes you need to get close to your dreams to realise they were only part of the journey.

I mentioned this earlier in the book, here is a further breakdown, the three A's of letting go.

This is one of the most powerful formulas you will find to

help release emotional and physical pains.

Accept – one of the best things you can do is accept you are in pain, stop all the fighting and pretending. Accept it.

Acknowledge – Acknowledge where you are carrying it; when it is physical it is a bit easier to recognise where it is; when it is emotional it can be a little harder. However, our bodies are amazing at letting us know when something needs addressing and where we are holding it. There it is important to acknowledge where you are holding any emotional pain. A simple scan works wonders. When I have done a body scan at my seminars, people very quickly realise where they are carrying the emotional pain and discover a little extra. After all, we are amazing storage vessels, we store emotional pain in our body, and it's important to acknowledge where it is because then it can be addressed.

Ask – This is where some magic lies. Being a peak performance coach, I hate fluffy impractical stuff. However, this is powerful beyond measure. The speed of your recovery or letting go depends on the strength of the questions you ask. Once you accept and acknowledge you ask:

- What is right about this that I am not getting?

- What is the message here?

- What is there to learn?

- How is this serving me?

This is where the magic begins. You are not asking your conscious mind, you are asking your deeper self. Here is some more magic: this is where your inner wisdom gives you the answer you need and everything around you will conspire to give you the answer you need. Here is the trick, you have to stay open and allow your unconscious mind to send you what you need to hear. That comes from repeatedly asking the questions. I would recommend you ask each question six times a day, sometimes twice a day, once in the morning and once in the evening for at least 21 days. Your inner wisdom will give you the answer you need once you clear the path by asking the right questions.

What will it take for you to adopt this approach?

Tip

When you carry around needless pain, you are blocking yourself spiritually, emotionally and physically, thus elongating the suffering. Don't wait till you are in full meltdown, you are getting messages on a daily basis and in order to listen apply the three A's every day.

To achieve consistent success and to maintain momentum, is about continual and never-ending growth fused with patience. I am aware a concept people fling around is The Law of Attraction. The key word in attraction is action, Attract Action = Attraction. The law doesn't discriminate, it will work depending on what you are focusing on and what belief systems are at play. However, it will only work for you if you are out there and in the action, countlessly growing and learning. A lot of people come from a place of entitlement and expect everything to land in their lap or have this deluded notion that they are owed something. It is true you will attract something in the form of frustration and heartache. The law of attraction can work in your favour if you play the odds:

- Work on your growth continuously

- Keep focusing on your outcome

- Keep reviewing and working on your beliefs system

- Stay grateful

- Keep taking action

- Allow time to do its thing, it's about long term results vs. short term gain

Remember the key word is ACTION.

Want to Become a Powerful Performer?

What I am going to share with you in the next chapter has come over years of experience, being a professional performer myself and through my coaching. What I have done is put together an easy structure for you to remember and to follow in order to increase performance. I have used this on clients, and we have used this method to measure and increase some businesses' productivity, which includes my time with a big broadband company across the UK and a large call centre to name a few.

These P's will help you along the way to mastering your journey and your craft. It is similar to when I got injured, it may have altered my route but not my destination. My destiny was to always impact and transform people's lives through whatever it is I do; now it is coaching.

I want to let you know upfront that you will hear different versions of this from various people. Here I will share what has worked for me. These five P's apply regardless if you are a creator, entrepreneur, business owner, athlete, etc. The principles are simple and can be applied to any field.

You may be wondering how they can apply to so many different fields. When you read through this chapter, you will see they apply to you regardless of the situation you are in. When you apply them, you will see a huge difference and be able to increase productivity. One rule:

you have to apply and take action.

Pain: as we have already discussed in the previous chapter, pain is a message telling us that something isn't right. Pain is a reminder that something needs addressing. If the pain is small, you can capture it in time and have time to address it. If the pain is big, you need to stop what you are doing before you do any more harm. The learning will be worth it. Always address the pain while it is still small and not big yet. And remember that pain is part of the process.

Think about when you get to the gym for the first time and you have a huge workout. In the middle your body hurts, you can't breathe and you feel dizzy. Know that feeling? You are breathing like your lungs are going to explode and your mind is saying stop. However, accepting the pain and keeping your eye on the bigger picture is what keeps you going. It is the same with following your passions and finding your path. There is, of course, another level, you have to seek the leaks along the way. That doesn't mean manifesting them or creating them. It means looking to see what the pain is within you and around in order to address it.

How does this apply to a business?

- Where are the pain points currently in the business?

- What isn't running smoothly?

- What needs addressing right away?

For Entrepreneurs:

- What pain are you addressing with the creation, service or business that you are building?

- Where is the pain for you around getting there?

- Where are your pain points in your journey that need addressing right away?

For an athlete:

- Where is the pain physically that is limiting you from moving up?

- What is the pain that needs addressing?

On a mental level,

- What's the pain you have around being a world-class athlete and successful?

- What pain blockages do you have emotionally?

Some general questions around Pain and how to assess it:

Where is the pain that needs addressing to get better results?

- Who needs you to address their pain?

- Where is the pain?

- Is the pain enough?

- Is it time to face the pain?

Most people avoid the last question; if you face your pain early, it isn't as much of a challenge.

As you can see, the questions can be asked from anyone at any stage in any place in the walk of life. I have chosen to use those areas to demonstrate the point because when you address the pain and keep going, deal with the challenge along the way, success awaits, lives and is ready to welcome you.

Practice – Are you practising everything in excellence? Are you showing up in excellence in all areas of your life? Are you giving what you say you will give? Are you delivering everything you say you will? Right now while I am writing this book, there is a little bit of a financial crisis out there. The companies that are surviving are those offering exceptional value and doing it excellently. We have seen my own business grow because I walk my walk and give massive value upfront. Wherever I show up, I make sure there is excellence both in mental attitude and appearance. I always go back to the basics and carry on training. I look at the basics of cash flow. I look at the basics of the clothes I am wearing. Sometimes we can get caught up in our hype and then we forget to go back to basics, do the little things that matter and practise what we preach.

When I was climbing my way to where I am today, I spent hours practising my craft, and I do mean hours, we are talking thousands of hours, and I still do it. Let's take my speaking, for example, it didn't happen overnight, and it is a never-ending journey. I always take time out to ensure I am drilling and maintaining high standards. I always listen to feedback about what I could do better and how I can improve. I would, and still do record each session and listen back so as to iron out any kinks. When I am travelling or sitting on the train, I listen to them time and time again. Within our business, we always review how we are showing up, positioning ourselves and executing our services. We practice excellence, we strive for it continually. After every event, we review what worked and what we could be doing better. We review my delivery. We review the slides we used. We review how the team did. We review the overall experience. We review the sales process. We review what I wore and all this in the name of excellence. We don't always get it right, and it doesn't always work. Then we take full responsibility and respond in excellence. Showing up in excellence isn't just when things are going well; in fact, it is far more important when things aren't going so smoothly. That's where excellence shows up and that's where credibility lives. We also always look and review the promises we offer and make sure we deliver. Adding massive value is our daily practice.

For a business:

- Do you practise what you preach?

- Do you deliver what you promise when you say you will?

- Are you practising being customer centred?

For an entrepreneur:

- Are you showing and practising making a difference through your innovation and being an entrepreneur?

- Are you delivering what you promise when you say you will?

For an athlete:

- Are you practising enough?

- Is your practice effective?

- Are you practising and striving for the next level?

By practising never-ending improvement and excellence, you will excel and you will become a powerful performer in any field.

Proactive and preventative – What lesson are you learning from the first two P's Pain and Practice, which you can proactively implement, and which will prevent you from recurring mistakes. Where can you implement measures so history doesn't repeat itself?

Being proactive about prevention is a massive part of becoming a peak performer. In the space of a month back in 2011, I lost my clients, spent all my money going to Australia, and didn't get paid what I was promised. Had I applied those two proactive preventions, I wouldn't have ended up in that mess. Had I actually spent more time investing in client attraction and feeding my pipeline, it would have been prevented because I would have new clients coming in all the time. Had I looked closer at the client's behaviour, I would have seen the writing on the wall, addressed the situation earlier, and I certainly would not have spent my hard-earned money on going to Australia for a month. I would have made sure I had more of a buffer financially. I would have made sure all the relationships I had were solid and found out my clients' intentions for the six months. I would have gone out for a shorter period. As a result of that pain, I am much more proactive about prevention.

We now review all the angles of a situation and look at best and worst-case scenarios. We plan for the best and the worst outcome. This isn't about manifesting it, this is about being prepared for all outcomes. There is everything right in this approach because it will allow you to predict and see the leaks if there are any. It will allow you to choose the best material to plug the leaks. If there are no leaks, then there is no harm done.

Hindsight is a great thing, which is why I can sit here and explain this to you. Most things in life are preventable. The attitude "it will be OK" is a dangerous one because you are surrendering yourself and disempowering yourself, hoping that it will work. I hoped it would work out too when I lost my clients, and I hoped that it would work out with the clients that would pay me the money I was owed. I not only hoped, I even fought for it. It didn't work out because I didn't proactively prevent what could have been.

Look at systems, processes that can be implemented to proactively prevent more pain. When you step up your game, you start to operate at a higher level energetically, emotionally and physically. Because you have been operating at a different level, the pain you will have to deal with will have greater impact. You will have to shoulder greater responsibility and pressure can appear greater. Unless, of course, you look to proactively prevent what could go wrong, keep looking at best and worst case scenarios. You see this all the time with people that hit success quickly. Their collapse appears to be as quick as their rise because they didn't take time to look at the pain proactively and be preventative. Just look at a lot of footballers who shoot to fame, once their football career is over, many of them go bust because they don't consider that the money might stop. A lot of wrestlers in the U.S., basketball players and people who win reality shows fall into this trap.

Personality – What personality do you have, and who do you want to become?

When I was turning everything around, I had to change my ways and look at developing a different type of personality. I had to become a go-to guy, for this I had to change my traits and belief system. I had to learn what other successful people did and how they dealt with challenge. I had to see myself as more than I was, bigger than I was and had to stop making it about me. I had to make it about something greater than me and give that a personality to match. My business has a personality of its own. My seminars have their personality. Personality plays a huge part in your peak performance. If you are applying this to the business:

- What is the personality of the business you are dealing with?

Dominant

The dominant personality type is the hard-working and objective-focused person who is sometimes referred to as the "choleric" personality type or even a "type A" personality. They are businesspersons who know how to achieve their goals and don't mind being straightforward and to the point in how they handle their employees and business relationships. These business leaders generally work with a high level of energy and are objective-driven, always trying to accomplish the next important business task.

Expressive

Expressive people are the ones who make natural salespeople and have the ability to use their extroversion to their advantage. The expressive business-persons are those who generally tend to be optimistic and competitive in their approach to business. These people are also high-energy types who are always on the go and are always willing and ready to accept the next challenge. These extroverts make great marketing professionals and even business trainers because of their outwardly obvious personality. They know how to establish business relationships and maintain them through their enthusiastic approach to business endeavours.

Introvert

Introverts are the exact opposite of the expressive personality type in business. These people are the analytical type, who think things through very carefully before acting. They tend not to be driven by emotion but rather by facts and data that help them make an informed business decision. They must know all the necessary details before making such a decision through careful deliberation. Although sometimes portrayed as the pessimist, the introvert simply prefers to be the voice of reason or the devil's advocate among co-workers and employers. They prefer to act in a rational manner and not make a business mistake.

Relational

The relational personality type is someone who is similar to the expressive type in that s/he is outwardly expressive – but only to a certain extent. These business-people are those who work best in group situations and are driven by their relationship with other employees. Even though driven by outward relations, this personality type does sometimes have an introverted side. They can be easygoing and will sometimes exhibit the "go with the flow" mentality that helps them avoid conflict in the business world. Because of this, the relational business-person tends to be a better follower in business matters, rather than a leader.[4]

- What is the personality of your customers?

- What is the personality you wish to develop for your journey as this will play a huge part in your growth, and what kind of team do you want to build around you? Really think what you want to be known for? What type of business do you want to build?

As an entrepreneur:

- Who is doing what you are doing and how can you learn from?

- How did they get there?

- How do they deal with challenge?

- If your journey was similar to that of a superhero, who would they be and why?

- How can you implement those traits in your own journey?

---

[4] http://smallbusiness.chron.com/four-types-business-personalities-26162.html

As an athlete:

- Who is your role model?

- How do they train?

- How do they present themselves?

- How can you be you and add-in those traits?

Other angles to consider:

- What traits do you need to develop to give you the personality that is needed?

- What do you want to be known as?

- What are people saying about you when you are not in the room?

- Would you recommend yourself and why?

- What is going to be your legacy?

Answer these questions to build or check in where you are heading. There is no right or wrong here. You can use it as a check and see if you are on track or not. Maybe you will find you are developing something that you don't like or weren't even thinking of? Really take the time to answer these questions as you might surprise yourself with the answers. Remember it is all about the action.

To sum up this chapter, the five P's to becoming a powerful peak performer are:

- Pain

- Practice

- Proactive and Prevent

- Personality

Start applying these today and let the results unfold.

The T's & C's of Success

Here are some key foundations to build upon in your journey. What I am going to share here is priceless. It is simple, effective and it works. Not only does it work, it works well. I would like to start with the three T's.

All three words are to do with one single principle: it is called trust. Nowadays, trust can be flung around like a smelly fish that no one wants. People behave toward trust like it stinks and is bad for you. How many times do you hear "don't trust anyone" or "every time I trust someone I get hurt." Really? Every time? And everyone? I don't think so. In fact, I know that isn't so. This isn't helped by people writing about not trusting anyone and people shouting about it on social media. Just think of all the areas where you might need trust:

- Business

- Friends

- Partners

- The higher Power

- The universe

- In yourself.

People underestimate the relationship between Trust and happiness; trust and running an effective and productive business; trust and having a flourishing relationship. People often forget that trust is a fundamental human experience. Trust plays a bigger part than we think in our everyday life. We need to trust for society to function. Trust is everything we do, which is why we get so pissed off when the banks let us down so badly because we trusted them with our money. We get annoyed when the trains are delayed because we trust that they will be on time. Trust plays a huge part in individual happiness. Without trust, fear rules! And all one needs to do is look around and see that it is true.

Here is a fact: unless you live on an island, you have to trust to a certain degree. A lot of people are uncertain about whom to trust, when to trust, how much to trust and if to trust at all. On a daily basis, we make choices about whom and how much to trust. We are always evaluating how much to trust someone, which can be a good thing to a certain degree.

A lot of people have a total lack of trust, which would indicate a serious psychological problem. Imagine waking every day not trusting and always watching your back, always feeling hard done by and that someone will have one over you. That is a life of uncertainty, fear and scarcity. Judgements about when and whom to trust help keep us alive, this is true; however, it can also keep us isolated and shut off. People mistake mistrust for being strong, and that is a very lonely place. I know, I used to live there.

In my experience of working with 100s of people, there are

some classic symptoms that show distrust:

- Always talking in the negative about outcomes, saying things like: things never work out, you can't trust these people, once bitten twice shy

- Shut down and closed off

- Relationships always start off nicely and then pull back, normally this happens suddenly

- Lots of drama around people screwing them over and continuous rocky and stormy relationships

- Continuous thoughts of suspicion or anxiety about opportunity, friends and family

- Strong belief that others are all deceptive with no real evidence, yet they are always looking to prove it.

If trust seems to play a dominant role in your outcomes and you seem to get burnt on a regular basis, there are various reasons why this happens. Yes, they might be deep rooted in your unconscious mind. It could be past disappointments or betrayals by friends, a family member, strangers screwing you over, to name a few.

In my search to further help people understand why that is and why they might attract this into their lives, I break it down to the following elements of trust, which are all a huge part of our foundation.

Trust yourself – whatever your past experiences, outcomes or thoughts around trust, you have to trust yourself first and foremost. People don't move forward because they don't trust themselves enough. You have the honour and privilege to be alive and have one of the most sophisticated computers in your head. You have the honour of waking up with yourself every day. You also have the honour of being part of the grand plan and are part of an amazing race called humans with all our faults. When you start to trust yourself, you carry around a stronger energy and certainty. It doesn't mean you will always get it right. However, you will be far more in control. How many times have you been in a situation where you knew the answer, but chose to ask someone else instead? Trust yourself!

Our brain is great at protecting us, as is our body. Know that if something feels right, it's good, and if something doesn't, find out what is behind it, explore why it doesn't feel right. Our inner wisdom has a way of letting us know when something isn't right. By all means ask around, but the most important thing is that you make the decision and you trust what is right for you. While everyone around wants what's best for you, they are living their lives and you have to live yours. Trust yourself. It is the trust in myself, in my work and the higher power that got me here. I didn't always get it right, but I always trust that I am getting what I need to learn to grow and go to the next level. Because I trust in myself, I own a lot of the decisions I make and the journey. I also attract great people around me who are trustworthy. Once again, I don't always get it right, just most of the time. Simply because I made a deep-rooted decision to trust myself despite everything that has happened. I had to ask how long am I willing to stay lonely and closed off? How far is far enough? Trust yourself.

Trust your team

One of our biggest fears is handing over something we might have built up to someone who isn't us. For some people, the train of thought is "I must do everything myself" or "If you want something done, do it yourself." This is a very old school way of thinking and seldom productive. You have to own everything you do and all the action you take. Remember this: you can't do it all! Anyone telling you otherwise is full of shit!

There is also no such thing as a self-made millionaire. Look at the likes of Branson, JK Rowling, Lady Gaga and even Barbie. Everyone has a team around them because when things grow you can't do everything alone, and if you do it won't be effective. You will burn out and your business or journey will suffer and collapse. Building a team around yourself and trusting them is one of the most important T's you will ever come across. Stop being a hero and start letting people help you. Did you know there are people out there who love doing spreadsheets? Who love being geeks, and maybe you are one of them. Now build and get people who love what you don't want to do and also are experts in that field. Surround yourself with little geniuses.

My business partner has great understanding. He doesn't

touch my speaking or presentation stuff, and I don't do any type of communications without him. Because that is what he does! He deals with contracts because he loves the details, and I build the relationships. The team doesn't have to be big. The great thing about a team is it can grow at your pace. We have certainly taken our time with it and will continue to do so. Once someone is on my team, I trust them to do the job, whatever it is. Edit a video, do the online marketing. You need different minds to progress the business, TRUST your team. When you trust yourself, you are able to trust other people. Whatever you do, don't take on another you. Take on someone that complements you and challenges you because that's where growth is born. It is part of the process. If you take on another you and build the team with people that won't speak back to you or challenge you then you might as well have a team of virtual assistants, hand them a task list and it will be done. That is not where success is, grows or is owned. If it weren't for my team at various times, I would have fallen on my face and back at a full-time job and hating it. The days of doing it alone are over. Trust the team.

Trust your community

The term community now has many different levels, which is why it is so important. Community in its origin is about a small village of people whose values are aligned. Community can also mean your family and close friends. Community can be your online following via social networks or through blogging. That's why the concept of trusting your community is so important because it can serve you on so many levels and you can actually get the community to do a lot of work for you.

Here is an important note: your community will do that because you give them so much value. Not because you own them or manipulate them, but for the simple reason that you give them so much value. By handing trust to your community, you are giving people permission to help spread your message. You're handing your community the ability to carry your work forward, talk about you and share whatever it is you do.

At the beginning, it will be you doing all the talking, and after you have proven yourself to be a worthwhile leader, innovator and success, your community will take over and help you spread the message.

I remember, at the beginning, I would have meeting after meeting with various people wanting them to help me get clients, or email their database or put me on their stage. To begin with, a lot of people simply didn't see the value I offer, and I didn't have my value proposition well-shaped. When I was speaking to people, they weren't going to risk what they have spent decades building. Slowly I started to get 10 minutes here and there. People started to like my message, but that still wasn't enough. I created products, went on Britain's Next Top Coach, came third, wrote a book, got a few more speaking slots. I supported other speakers both to show face as well as to learn from them. I wrote another book, created some more products, and became a facilitator for another training company. Then my 10 minutes became 30, then 45 to an hour. I kept working on my elevator pitch and still do. I went to various networking events to get myself out there. I would have a meeting with people for coffee and so they got to know me better. I did taster sessions till I got to the point where I valued my time too much and started to charge. I started my own seminars; I tested different ways of doing it, different pricing strategies. We rebranded and changed the name to *POWER TO SUCCEED*. Let me explain why we did it, maybe you might need to do a review of your brand too? The seminar used to be called *It's Your Right To Be Wrong*, which is the name of my first book. We weren't pulling the numbers, and I was wondering why. We sat down with a marketing consultant, a cool guy from New Zealand called Glen. Glen took us through half a day of form filling and question answering, and then delivered the key outcome from the afternoon. "Guys, no one wants to go to a seminar to be told they are wrong! Change the name." This is why it is important to get the right people in. That evening, I went home and discussed the notion with Emily, my fiancé and Andrew, a good friend. We discussed everything we covered at *Power to Succeed* and the key learnings people get. We did some word play with different names. Power to … Success Summit … Succeed without Limit … and then Emily simply came out with it. POWER TO SUCCEED that's what the seminar does and from that day *It's Your Right To Be Wrong* was renamed *Power To Succeed*. It had a makeover, it went from a one-day to two-day programme and has grown in numbers ever since.

Once I had done all that, I started to build a community around me. The community has built up more because I got people results and added value to their lives, whether it would be in their businesses or personal lives, and freed them from trauma or gave them action steps to get going. There have been many, you have heard about Carl, Eve, Nami, Flo, Beatrix, and those are just a handful of clients.

Ruth came to me after being made redundant from a tax firm. She was lost, hurt and directionless. We worked together to build her business, which she has done. She now runs a tax company and it is in year four and growing every year. In the community, we have lawyers, dentists, aerospace engineers, artists, makeup artists, chefs, raw food chefs, authors, skin care product designers, photographers, accountants, massage therapists, coaches, nurses, social workers, youth workers, teachers, network marketers, image consultants, property investors and many more. Because I added massive value, now people want to send emails to me, they want to sit down and have coffee with me and want to share my message. Now I do talks lasting anything from an hour, two hours to two days. However, I will say this, the work is never done. I still do pretty much most speaking gigs that I am asked to do, and I still sit down and have coffee with people. I also still follow up with various clients to see how they are getting on. Where can you do more to connect with people?

Because I trust my community, I trust the right people will spread the message. I trust my community of family members that support me in this journey. I trust the community of higher powers that be that they have my back and when challenge comes along that they want me to learn a lesson. The rewards will come. As long as in your community you trust and keep talking and telling the world about you and what you do.

As you have had the three T's of success – Trust yourself, Trust your team and Trust Your Community – we will now move on to the C's of success.

As you will find, everything intertwines. The five C's are something we use to build and reshape businesses. The C's also apply to your everyday life, but they are so important in your journey, they could be the difference between success and non-success. Here is the amazing part, they are so simple.

The first C is Coach

Now, of course, being a coach I will mention coaching. I will always recommend you have a coach and a coaching force in your life. This C is about you becoming a coach; that you coach the people around you how to communicate with you, how to respond to you and how to interact with you. You step into the role of coach. We see it all the time around us. We are always being coached how to use Facebook, Twitter, etc. The global brands are always coaching us on how to use them and how to interact with them. The interaction doesn't happen by accident. It happens because the people who want to interact with them, buy from them and become loyal to them are always coaching you. This is why it is important you become a coach and coach people on how to interact with you. Because you coach, the community that you build is the next C. All this while having a coach yourself, of course.

Community

The community now more than ever is important in your journey. These are the people that you coach on how to respond. These are the people that will buy your products and tell others. We discuss community in the Trust section. This is still important to address. The community is everything in your journey. Would you say that Facebook has a community and that there is more and more importance being placed on building a community around you? This is because these are your customers. However, your communities are your advocates and your raving fans, the people that will tell people about you and what you do. They will cheer you on and be there for you even if you have never physically seen them. This will happen because you added so much value to them. Here is the catch, you build a community for you to serve and be of service to, not because you want to be worshipped. You build a community because you want to transform and solve a problem for people. You know who builds communities around them for the sole purpose of survival and so they can keep going at the expense of others? Parasites!

Therefore, being on this path is of service, being of service to your community and to your success.

Collaboration

A collaborative mindset and approach accelerate results. By collaborating you look for and will find people to work with, which means together you grow faster. Collaboration is the new currency and how business is conducted. It is about finding people who align with your values and vision to create a win-win path so you both grow.

Connection

Without connection, how will people buy from you? Get to know you? And how will you form good long-lasting relationships? Connection is an essential part of your growth, connection is how people get to know what you are all about. It's time to surface from the shadows of social media and truly connect with people. Look them in the eye, discuss things face to face, not hidden behind a screen. Connection is one of our human needs and often a key one we neglect. Look to see how you can connect better with people as human beings and how you can add value to their lives.

Consistency

This is what glues everything together, it is doing and taking action on a consistent basis. Going back again and again. Learning, growing and showing up every time. It means that when things don't work out you keep going, it means that when things are working you look for the next level. Do you know why the graveyard is the wealthiest place on this planet? It is because people take their dreams with them to the grave because they gave up too soon. By virtue of being consistent, you will create results. It is consistently understanding there is always another level and that it is a never-ending journey.

When you play the role of a coach and become a coaching force, you build a community to serve, which then starts to collaborate and remains connected to you, your journey and their path. You add value consistently, watch everything around you accelerate. There is something magical and powerful about the five C's.

This whole book is about long-term gain and not short-term satisfaction. It's about being a living breathing example of the Ts&Cs of success, implanting the tools as and when you need them and educating others on their greatness through you achieving yours. Take action, learn and reflect. Build your path and your future the way you want to live and by your high standards. Take the next step and join us live. Keep growing and carry on investing in your journey. After all, at the end of the day, what we leave behind is our legacy. What will yours be?

Here's What You Can Achieve in 3 Months

This guy approached me at one of the events I was running. 'I need your help!' he said.

'Why?' I asked.

'Well, I have had my proposal for a new App. accepted and I have never done any public speaking.'

'None?' I asked.

'Nope' he responded. 'My name is Alexander Ball.'

'Nice to meet you. How do you feel about pitching?' I asked.

Alex's response was: 'I am shitting myself and this is well out of my comfort zone. I find it hard to speak in meetings with two people, let alone pitching in front of an audience.'

Do you know that feeling? The feeling when your hands get sweaty, your heart races, and suddenly the sound of your own voice sounds strange? And the voices in your head are saying things like: I must sound like I don't know what I am talking about, everyone looks really bored … ooops, what if I get it wrong … aaaarrrggghhhhhh … know that feeling? That's what Alex went through every time he got up to speak. I then asked him who was the target audience and what was the deal? It turned out it was for one of the biggest banks globally and it would be a three-round pitch and at each round you must be chosen to go through to the next. The first one would be four minutes in a small room in front of the Lions (Their version of Dragons' Den or Shark Tank); the second one would be for eight minutes and the last round would be in Holland in front of 500 people.

Challenge accepted, the work started. We started with a one-to-one session where we looked at structuring the pitch. We carefully looked at the types of words to use for massive impact and how to explain what the App does. We went through it again, again and again for three hours, repeatedly tweaking and adapting. People don't succeed because they can't, people don't succeed because they stop too soon or give up. At times I could see Alex getting angry and frustrated, and at one point he really got angry. I stopped him and asked: 'You do care about this pitch don't you? And you want this really badly don't you?' 'Of course I do!' he responded. 'Then use this anger to drive this pitch forward. You have a real chance here to create impact, a chance of a lifetime. When you next pitch at me, come from that place of anger and let your passion out.' The pitch changed completely! His tone changed, it had meaning and passion. End of Session One.

'Go home and practise it at least 50 times a day, make it happen,' I told him. We then had a catch up call over Skype and Alex looked good and ready. It was over to him – was he going to do it? Was he going to deliver? Do you sometimes feel that way?

In my heart, I knew he would. The question was: did *he* believe it? One thing we did during the first session was every time he got flustered and nervous, we agreed he would remind himself that this App. wasn't about him, it was about the lives it would impact and he would put himself aside.

To bring you into the loop, the App. he wanted to build was to offer financial education to young people from 8 to 18, replacing the piggy bank. Besides that, I can't tell you anything else.

The day arrived and Alex was going up. It just happened to be a lovely day in London. The sun was shining and I was busy working on new branding. At the back of my mind, I was wondering how Alex was getting on. After all, my clients' results are my results. 'How is he doing?' is the thought that kept popping into my mind. Then at the end of the day, finally I got the text: **I am through!** I did a few fist pumps and it was celebration time. We both knew celebrations couldn't last too long. Now, we had more work to do.

We booked in the next session. This time we had to double the time, yet still be impactful and precise. We started to pull the pitch out. I introduced him to the Million Pound Concept, which is: if you had to pay a million pounds for every word you said, you would only choose impactful words, right? What was interesting was that he showed me the cost of building this App. Alex was pitching for a million Euros. This became a million Euro pitch.

Again we scripted, practised, tweaked, changed, changed and changed again until we were happy with the pitch. We kept his sights on the big picture and also what it would mean for him to get through to the final. By the way, Alex runs marathons and pitching this App. scared him far more. Again, it was over to him to practise, which of course he did. The stakes were high and he had everything to gain.

While Alex was pitching this round, I was in America. I was out both delivering training and attending training. We were doing long days. Sleep was something that we I was looking forward to every day. I had finally fallen asleep when I got the text: **I am through to the final! We need to talk and get this ready to present in front of 500 people.** 'Great news!" I thought, 'I'd better get some sleep!'

Within a day, we very quickly jumped on Skype and arranged everything. In the meantime, I said, 'I want you to go over the pitch, put yourself in the shoes of someone listening to it, and ask: What's so good about that? What's in it for me? And why should I care? These are great questions to ask yourself when you are talking about any type of product or pitch.'

Alex, being the hard worker that he is, did exactly that. We met once I was back from the USA and worked on his final pitch. We also worked on adding some stage anchoring, gestures, and getting him moving around. We also added music to the pitch, as that was part of the requirement for the big pitch. We worked on everything and it was his moment. I felt a bit like the football manager who has set all the tactics and game plan, then it is over to the players. It was over to him, to conquer his fear, to deliver his pitch, and to be awarded a million pounds in funding. Have you been in that place where you just know it is time for you to truly step up and deliver?

One thing we discussed while preparing was to remember that he had earned his spot and he had every right to be there and to pitch along with anyone else on that stage. Not from a place of arrogance, but from a place of self-recognition. He had worked very hard and needed to acknowledge it for himself as this would eliminate the "who am I to do this?" mindset. This was very important.

I had asked if I could fly out with him to support him at his big pitch. He was told, no. The big day came. He flew out a couple of days before. We were texting each other. I kept thinking, 'This is his big moment. He is ready. He will own this.' We also agreed that the day before, the best thing he could do was simply relax. The day came. Alex got on stage and delivered the pitch of a lifetime. By this point, I was back in the UK again. This time, I kept thinking about Alex a lot more: 'Will he get the million Euros? Will he deliver? How will he cope with 500 people and the Lions asking him tough questions?' I had no idea what time he was on. I kept looking at my watch: 'Has he done it yet?' An hour later: 'Has he done it yet?' Then a few more hours passed. 'Surely he has done it now!' Nothing. My phone was blank, no text, nothing, not a peep. Then, at 19:46pm, the text came through... **We WON.** I was so happy for him, so happy as well as relieved. I had had my own little nervous journey for him. Now I could smile and relax. Alex had done it.

Yet this turned out to be only the beginning for Alex, which is why I decided to write this only *after* my book was finished.

Since raising the money, Alex is learning what it is like to be a leader and steering an international team globally. He is finding doors that were closed for him opening now. He is called into meetings all the time to do the pitch and people are offering their support to the project. He recently got offered a 6-month placement in Amsterdam to work with the innovation team and is still deciding if he will do it or not. He has found that he is seen in a different way now. Alex is one of the most humble people I know and he certainly does not crave attention. To see him deal with it for me is very interesting.

The reason I wanted to add this in is because I want you to ask yourself some very serious questions:

- Where are you missing out on opportunities because you allow head stuff to get in the way?

- Where are you making the fear to be bigger than the action?

- Where are you allowing yourself to play small?

- Where are you not expressing yourself in order not to rock the boat?

If Alex had let his fear win, if Alex hadn't reached out to ask for support, and if Alex hadn't taken massive action, this would have been another faded dream. Another good idea gone to waste and another opportunity missed.

Where are you doing the same? Are you letting your dreams fade away? What if today you committed to yourself to do things differently?

Come Join Us Live

Thank you from the bottom of my heart for choosing to read this book all the way through. What was your greatest lesson from reading this book? I feel like now you have read this book, we are kindred souls. I want to carry on this journey together and take it a step deeper and further. As you have read this book, come and join me live at my seminar *Power To Succeed*, where you will get a live experience and more life-changing experiences. Let's go to the next level together. Wouldn't that be great?

To get your discount for the next *Power To Succeed* go to: **www.powertosucceedtoday.com** and insert this code: ptsbook2015disc

You will get a surprise discount and be able to find out more about where I am speaking next. When you come along, make sure that you come over and say hi, after all connection is one of my most important values. See you at the next *Power To Succeed*. Do it today as they get booked up fast.

Printed in Great Britain
by Amazon